KITCHEN
TABLE

100 Vegetarian Feasts
SOPHIE GRIGSON

www.mykitchentable.co.uk

Welcome to MY KITCHEN TABLE

I've always believed that vegetables, grains, herbs and spices are the most interesting and exciting foodstuffs to cook with. They offer **an incredible range of flavours, colours and textures**. No meat? No problem.

Sophie Grey

Contents

Fresh Vegetable Stock

Most vegetable stock recipes are just meat stocks without the meat, which makes them insipid and unbalanced. When I make vegetable stock I include potatoes and mushrooms to contribute 'umami', that essential savoury taste, as well as a tomato to introduce a touch of acidity to balance the sweetness of carrots, leeks and onions. This makes a cloudy stock, which is fine for most recipes, just not a glistening limpid consommé.

Step one Put all the ingredients into a large pan with 1.5 litres (2½ pints) cold water. Bring to the boil, then reduce the heat, cover with a lid and simmer very gently for 30 minutes.

Step two Strain the stock through a fine sieve, pressing the ingredients against the sides of the sieve to extract all the liquid. Leave to cool completely, then chill in a covered container for up to 3 days before use.

This stock can be frozen for up to 3 months.

Makes about 1 litre (1¾ pints)

1 leek, thickly sliced

1 large carrot, thickly sliced

2 celery sticks, thickly sliced

1 onion, roughly chopped

75g (3oz) button, chestnut or open-cup mushrooms, quartered

1 medium potato, thickly sliced

1 tomato, quartered

3 fresh parsley sprigs

2 bay leaves

4 fresh thyme sprigs

Lovage, Potato and Carrot Soup

It is worth growing lovage for soup alone (though there's plenty more to be made of it than that). This soup is thick and warming and nicely spiced with the celery taste of lovage. I like it just as it is, eaten with a hunk of bread, but for a thinner, more elegant version, use stock rather than water, diluting it with a little extra at the end.

Serves 4–6

1 onion, chopped

4 large carrots, chopped

2 large potatoes, chopped

4 garlic cloves, chopped

zest, pared in strips, and juice of ½ lemon

4 tbsp roughly chopped fresh lovage leaves

25g (1oz) butter

1.2–1.8 litres (2–3 pints) vegetable stock (see page 7) or water

1 tomato, skinned, seeded and chopped

salt and pepper

Step one Sweat the onion, carrots, potatoes, garlic, lemon zest and lovage in the butter in a covered pan for about 15 minutes, stirring once or twice. Add 1.2 litres (2 pints) of stock or water, plus the tomato and some salt and pepper. Bring to the boil and simmer for about 20–30 minutes, until all the vegetables are very tender.

Step two Liquidize in batches, adding extra stock if you want a thinner soup, then stir in the lemon juice. Taste and adjust the seasoning and serve.

Float a spoonful of whipped cream speckled with some extra chopped fresh lovage or snipped fresh chives on each bowl of soup as it is served and it will look pretty and stylish.

KITCHEN TABLE

Have you made this recipe? Tell us what you think at www.mykitchentable.co.uk/blog

Gazpacho

When made with good tomatoes, this is perfect for a hot summer's day.

Step one In a large bowl, stir together all the vegetables, the vinegar and the breadcrumbs. Place a quarter of the mixture into a liquidizer with the tomato juice, 1 tablespoon of olive oil, salt, pepper, a pinch or two of sugar and a dash of iced water, if necessary. Liquidize until smooth, then repeat with the remaining ingredients, each time adding about 150ml (¼ pint) of icy cold water instead of the tomato juice. Mix the whole lot together, then taste and adjust the seasoning, adding a little more salt, vinegar or sugar as necessary to highlight the flavours.

Step two Chill, and adjust the seasoning again just before serving. Choose as many or as few of the garnishes as you like, place them in small bowls and pass around for people to help themselves.

Serves 6

700g (1½ lb) ripe, richly flavoured tomatoes, skinned, seeded and roughly chopped

¾ cucumber, peeled and roughly chopped

1 large green pepper, seeded and roughly chopped

2 garlic cloves, roughly chopped

½ red onion, chopped

2 2½ tbsp red wine vinegar or sherry vinegar

110g (4oz) fresh white breadcrumbs

150ml (¼ pint) tomato juice

4 tbsp extra-virgin olive oil

½–1 tsp sugar

salt and freshly ground black pepper

to serve

tomatoes, skinned, seeded and diced

cucumber, diced

red onion, diced

green pepper, seeded and diced

jamón serrano, diced

hard-boiled egg, shelled and chopped

Antonio Carluccio's Stracciatella all'Aglio (Garlic Soup)

Stracciatella is a marvellous Italian soup made with a good, flavourful stock and then lightly thickened with eggs and cream. *Aglio* (garlic) is the key ingredient. Antonio Carluccio, who uses garlic with gleeful abandon, showed me how to make his favourite version of *stracciatella* – I suspect that he might consider a mere half dozen cloves a weakling's dose, but to me it tastes just right. If you want to add more, however, that's absolutely fine.

Serves 4–6

1 litre (1¾ pints) very good vegetable stock (see page 7)

6 garlic cloves, very finely sliced

4 egg yolks plus 2 whole eggs

6 tbsp double cream

salt and pepper

to serve

4–6 slices of country or ciabatta bread, 1.5cm (about ½ in) thick, well toasted

2 garlic cloves, cut in half

extra-virgin olive oil

freshly grated Parmesan

1 small bunch of fresh chives, snipped

Step one Bring the stock to the boil in a saucepan, then add the slices of garlic and boil for 3–5 minutes.

Step two Meanwhile, rub each slice of bread with the cut side of a garlic clove, then drizzle about 1 teaspoon of olive oil over it. Pile the slices of bread up on a warm plate.

Step three In a bowl, beat the egg yolks and whole eggs together, then whisk in the double cream. Season. Pour the egg mixture into the boiling soup, whisking the soup constantly. Quickly draw the pan off the heat, whisk for a few seconds more, and the soup is done.

Step four Pour the soup into individual serving bowls and sprinkle thickly with Parmesan. Place the bread on the soup, pressing it down a little so that it soaks up some of the broth. Sprinkle with the chives and serve immediately.

Tomato, Sweetcorn and Basil Soup with Pesto Croûtons

This soup can serve as a first course but I usually make it the mainstay of a light lunch or supper. It looks very pretty and is immensely satisfying.

Step one Preheat the oven to 190°C/375°F/gas 5. If using fresh corn, stand the ear upright on the work surface and slice downwards with a sharp knife to take off the kernels.

Step two To make the soup, chop the onion and garlic and gently fry in the olive oil until tender, then add the tomatoes, tomato purée, sweetcorn and bouquet garni. Bring to the boil, then simmer until reduced by about a third. Add the stock or water and salt and pepper and bring to the boil. Simmer gently for about 10 minutes.

Step three Meanwhile, make the croûtons. Slice the bread into rounds about 1cm (½in) thick, brush both sides of the slices with olive oil and place on a baking sheet. Bake for about 20 minutes, turning occasionally, until golden brown.

Step four While the bread is baking, make the pesto. Put the basil leaves, cheese, pine nuts and garlic into a food processor and process to a paste. With the blades still running, trickle in enough olive oil to give a creamy sauce. Spread the baked bread with the pesto and top each one with a small dollop of crème fraîche, if using. Shortly before serving, shred the basil finely.

Step five When the soup is ready, remove the bouquet garni and liquidize about half the soup for a slightly chunky, knobbly texture or the whole lot for a smooth(ish) texture. Taste and adjust the seasoning, then reheat and stir in the shredded basil. Serve immediately, with the pesto croûtons in a bowl so that people can float their own on top if they wish to or keep them separate.

Serves 4–6

3 ears of corn, or 350g (12oz) frozen sweetcorn kernels, defrosted

1 large onion

3 garlic cloves

3 tbsp extra-virgin olive oil

2 x 400g (14oz) tins of chopped tomatoes

2 tbsp tomato purée

1 bouquet garni of fresh thyme, bay leaf and parsley sprigs

1 litre (1¾ pints) vegetable stock or water (see page 7)

a handful of fresh basil leaves

salt and pepper

for the pesto croûtons

½ stick French bread

75g (3 oz) fresh basil leaves

60g (2oz) pecorino or Parmesan

50g (2oz) pine nuts

2–3 garlic cloves, roughly chopped

110–125ml (3½–4fl oz) extra-virgin olive oil, plus extra for brushing

3 tbsp crème fraîche (optional)

15

Cucumber and Sorrel Soup

The combination of cucumber and sorrel – not so much sorrel that it overwhelms the more delicate taste of cucumber but enough to liven things up – works well in a summer soup. I think it is best served hot, but if you prefer to make a chilled version to serve on a warm day, use a couple of tablespoons of oil instead of the butter.

Serves 4

1 onion, chopped

40g (1½ oz) butter

1 large cucumber, peeled and diced

2½ tbsp pudding rice

1 bay leaf

1 fresh thyme sprig

1.2 litres (2 pints) vegetable stock (see page 7)

a handful of fresh sorrel (about 40–50g/ 1½–2oz), larger stalks removed, shredded

salt and pepper

to garnish

1 tomato, seeded and diced

fresh snipped chives

Step one Sweat the onion in the butter in a covered pan for 5 minutes, then add two-thirds of the cucumber, the rice, bay leaf and thyme. Stir, cover again and cook for a further 5 minutes. Add the stock and some salt and pepper, bring to the boil and simmer for about 10 minutes, until the rice is tender.

Step two Pick out and discard the bay leaf and thyme sprig. Stir in the sorrel, then liquidize in batches to form a smooth cream. Taste and adjust the seasoning.

Step three To serve, reheat gently, without boiling, then scatter the remaining cucumber, the tomato dice and some snipped chives over the top.

To enrich the soup a little, float a swirl of whipped cream, or drizzle some single cream, on the top of each bowl of soup just before serving.

Roast Garlic with Herbs

A whole head of garlic per person? Yes, that's right. Whenever I've dished up this first course, my guests have looked horrified at first, but they are soon tucking in gleefully, occasionally complaining that there are no seconds! It has to be eaten with the fingers, so provide plenty of napkins.

Step one Preheat the oven to 160°C/325°F/gas 3. Neaten up the heads of garlic by removing any loose pieces of papery skin. Trim the roots. Using a sharp knife, cut the papery skin off the top of the garlic, just exposing the very tips of the cloves.

Step two Place the garlic heads in small ovenproof dish and pour 6 tablespoons of water around them. Drizzle olive oil over the garlic heads and tuck the rosemary and thyme around them. Sprinkle with coarse salt. Cover the dish with foil and bake for 30 minutes. Uncover and bake for a further 15–30 minutes, basting occasionally with the juices, until the garlic is tender and yields when pressed. Add a little extra water if it is drying out.

Step three In a bowl, beat the goats' cheese with the herbs and salt and pepper to taste, then pile it into a clean bowl.

Step four Serve each person with a head of garlic and some of the herby cooking oil, slices of toast, napkins and a finger bowl. Using their fingers, guests should squeeze the individual creamy cloves of garlic like tubes of toothpaste onto their toast, drizzle with the herby oil, and eat with a dab of herby goats' cheese.

Serves 4

4 heads of garlic

6 tbsp extra-virgin olive oil

2 fresh thyme sprigs

2 fresh rosemary sprigs

coarse salt

to serve

2 x 150g (5oz) young fresh goats' cheese

a handful of fresh herbs (e.g. basil, flat-leaf parsley, chives, chervil), finely chopped (optional)

slices of rye bread or other good bread, lightly toasted

salt and freshly ground black pepper

Socca (Roasted Chickpea Pancake)

Socca is the street pancake of Nice, sold from great big metal dishes, hot and salty, with the golden tan of the chickpea flour browned and crisp at the edges, soft and tender inside.

Serves 4–6

150g (5oz) chickpea flour

1 level tsp salt

3 tbsp extra-virgin olive oil, for roasting

½ level tbsp finely chopped fresh rosemary leaves (optional)

freshly ground black pepper

Step one Sift the chickpea flour and the salt into a bowl. Make a well in the middle. Whisk in 370ml (13fl oz) water, a little at a time, to form a thin smooth batter. Leave to rest for 1–2 hours.

Step two Preheat the oven to 220°C/425°F/gas 7. Spoon the oil into a 24 x 31cm (9½ x 12½in) roasting tin and heat in the oven for 3–4 minutes. Stir the chickpea batter once more and then pour into the hot tin, scatter over the rosemary, if using, and return immediately to the oven. Bake for 10–15 minutes until the mixture is set and brown around the edges.

Step three Remove the tin from the oven and season the pancake with black pepper. Let it stand for 5 minutes, then cut into squares or strips, or just tear up and serve.

KITCHEN TABLE

For more recipes from My Kitchen Table, sign up for our newsletter at www.mykitchentable.co.uk/newsletter

Grilled Aubergine Sandwich with Mascarpone and Sun-dried Tomatoes

We filmed the titles for the television series *Taste of the Times* one chilly November day, popping in and out of shops and calling at food stalls along the length of London's Portobello Road and the adjoining Goldborne Road (a Mecca for anyone who likes Moroccan or Portuguese food). At lunchtime, we found ourselves under the flyover, where the best of the market ends, and dived into the Portobello Café for a quick lunch. The grilled aubergine sandwich with mascarpone and sun-dried tomatoes, sluiced down by a big mug of very British tea, was exactly what I needed to get me through the rest of the day.

Step one If you have time, salt the slices of aubergine lightly and leave for 30–60 minutes to degorge. Preheat the grill. Wipe the aubergine dry, then brush with olive oil and grill under the grill, fairly close to the heat, until browned on both sides and tender. Leave to cool slightly.

Step two Spread the mascarpone on the cut sides of the ciabatta, or on one side of each slice of bread. Season with salt and pepper. Sandwich the aubergine and the sun-dried tomatoes between the pieces of bread. Eat quickly, while still warm.

Serves 1

2 aubergine, cut lengthways into slices about 2cm (¾in) thick

extra-virgin olive oil

2 heaped tbsp mascarpone

⅓–½ ciabatta loaf, split in half and warmed through in the oven, or 2 large slices of sturdy pain de campagne or sourdough bread, lightly toasted

4 sun-dried tomato halves, cut into strips

salt and lots of freshly ground black pepper

23

Patatas Bravas

Patatas bravas, cubes of fried potatoes moistened with a chilli and tomato sauce, is one of the most popular of Spanish tapas. The chillied tomato sauce can also be made in advance and reheated when needed.

Serves 4

3 tbsp extra-virgin olive oil

2 medium–large waxy potatoes (e.g. Cara, large salad potatoes or larger new potatoes), total weight about 600g (1¼ lb), peeled and cut into 2cm (¾in) cubes

coarse sea salt

chopped fresh flat-leaf parsley, to serve

for the chillied tomato sauce

2 tbsp extra-virgin olive oil

½ onion, chopped

2 garlic cloves, chopped

450g (1lb) fresh tomatoes, chopped

1 bay leaf

1 fresh thyme sprig

2 fresh parsley stems

1 tbsp tomato purée

3 tbsp dry white wine

¼ tsp dried chilli flakes

½ tsp caster sugar

salt and freshly ground black pepper

Step one To make the sauce, heat the olive oil in a pan and add the onion and garlic. Fry over a moderate heat until the onion is tender. Add the tomatoes and fry for a further 5–6 minutes, until cooked down to a soft mass. Next, add the herbs, tied together to make a bouquet garni, the tomato purée, wine, chilli flakes, sugar, salt and pepper. Add 50ml (2fl oz) water and bring gently to the boil. Cover the pan and simmer quietly for about 30 minutes; then remove the bouquet garni. If you prefer a smooth sauce, rub it through a sieve. Reheat when needed.

Step two Heat the olive oil in a wide frying pan over a moderately high heat. Add the potatoes, and sauté, keeping them moving most of the time, for about 15 minutes, until crisp on the outside, tender on the inside. Drain briefly on kitchen paper.

Step three Serve the potatoes as soon as they are cooked: pile them on to a warm serving dish and then spoon about half of the sauce over them. Sprinkle with a little chopped parsley and salt and perch a pot of cocktail sticks on the side of the dish, so that people can spear chunks of potato, bathed in prickly hot tomato sauce. Serve the remainder of the sauce in a small jug or bowl so that people can help themselves.

I much prefer the texture of sautéed potatoes but they demand fairly constant attention for a quarter of an hour. Roasting the potatoes in the oven will make life a great deal simpler. Preheat the oven to 200°C/400°C/gas 6. Toss the potato cubes with the olive oil and some coarse salt and spread out in a single layer in a baking sheet. Bake for about 30–40 minutes until cooked through to a soft centre, but crisp on the outside. Don't try to turn them over for the first 20 minutes – they'll just stick.

Falafel with Tahina Cream in Pitta

Falafel are taking sandwich bars by storm, but if you want to taste them at their best make your own from dried chickpeas, not tinned. You'll soon be totally hooked.

Step one Chop the onion, garlic and coriander or parsley.

Step two Dry-fry the coriander and cumin seeds and then grind to a powder. Drain the chickpeas and place in a food processor with the spices and all the remaining falafel ingredients, except the oil. Process until smooth. Break off a knob and fry until browned. Taste and adjust the seasoning. Leave for 1 hour.

Step three Meanwhile, make the tahina cream. Put the crushed garlic into a bowl with the tahina. Beat in the lemon juice, then gradually beat in enough water to give a consistency of double cream. Don't worry when at first the tahina seizes up like concrete. Season with salt and add a touch more lemon juice. Pour into a serving bowl and dust lightly with cayenne pepper.

Step four Roll the falafel mixture into balls no bigger than a small walnut. Heat a large pan of oil to a temperature of 180°C/350°F (to test, drop a cube of bread in – it should immediately fizz and begin to brown within about 15 seconds). Deep-fry the falafel in batches until well browned. Drain on kitchen paper.

Step five While the falafel are cooking, heat the pitta bread in the oven. Put the tomatoes, cucumber and lettuce into bowls on the table, with the tahina cream. When the falafel are done, arrange on a plate with the coriander and wedges of the lemon.

Step six Let everyone fill their pitta with a few cubes of tomato, a shred or two of lettuce and a squeeze of lemon juice. Then a few falafel, followed by a drizzle of tahina cream, more tomato, lettuce, some cucumber, coriander and a little more lemon juice, salt and pepper and, finally, another slather of tahina cream.

Serves 8

for the falafel

225g (8oz) dried chickpeas, soaked in cold water for 24 hours

2 tsp coriander seeds

1 tbsp cumin seeds

1 small onion

2 garlic cloves

3 tbsp chopped fresh coriander or parsley

1 tbsp flour

¼ tsp baking powder

sunflower oil, for deep-frying

for the tahina cream

2 garlic cloves, crushed

175g (6oz) light tahina paste

juice of 1½ lemons

salt and cayenne pepper

to serve

8 pitta bread

4 tomatoes, cubed

½ cucumber, sliced

6 lettuce leaves, shredded

fresh coriander leaves

2 lemons, quartered

salt and freshly ground black pepper·   27

Deep-fried Potato Skins with Blue Cheese and Lovage Dipping Sauce

Whenever you make mashed potatoes, bake or microwave the potatoes (you'll get a better, fluffier mash that way, anyway) and save the skins. Next day, you can either bake or deep-fry them to make a very moreish pile of crisp skins to serve with a blue cheese dipping sauce.

Serves 4

skins from about 1kg (2¼ lb) baked potatoes, cut into triangles or rectangles, about 4–5cm (1½–2in) across

sunflower oil

salt

for the dipping sauce

75–110g (3–4oz) mild to medium-strong blue cheese (e.g. dolcelatte, Danish blue or gorgonzola)

about 6 tbsp thick soured cream

2–3 tbsp chopped fresh lovage leaves

1 tbsp lemon juice

salt and pepper

Step one If you are going to bake the potato skins rather than deep-fry them, preheat the oven to 220°C/425°F/gas 7. To make the dipping sauce, mash the blue cheese with a little of the soured cream until smooth, then gradually beat in the remaining cream. Stir in the lovage, lemon juice, salt and pepper. Taste and adjust the seasoning.

Step two To bake the potato skins, toss them in oil, working it over the skins with your fingers so that they are evenly coated, then spread out on a baking sheet and bake for about 8–12 minutes, until browned and crisp.

Step two (alternative) To deep-fry the potato skins, heat the oil to 180°C/350°F (to test, drop a cube of bread or a small piece of potato skin into the oil – if it immediately starts to fizz and begins to brown within about 15 seconds, then the heat is right) and fry the skins until golden brown, turning once or twice so that they are evenly cooked. Don't fry too many at a time or you will lower the temperature of the oil and end up with greasy results. When they are done, scoop out the potato skins with a slotted spoon and drain briefly on kitchen paper.

Step three Sprinkle the freshly baked or deep-fried potato skins with salt and serve piping hot with the blue cheese dipping sauce.

If you can't get lovage, try making this sauce with chives or parsley instead.

Pinzimonio (Italian Vegetable Dip)

Pinzimonio is the pretty name for one of the simplest Italian starters. It also happens to be extremely good, as long as your vegetables are very fresh (this is definitely not an occasion for buying up past-sell-by-date vegetables at a knockdown price). Prepare them no more than an hour or so in advance and store in sealed plastic bags in the fridge until nearly ready to use. The 'dip' is a DIY affair – each of you makes up his or her own mixture of olive oil, lemon juice, salt and pepper. If you are feeling flush, the lemon juice can be replaced with balsamic vinegar.

Step one Shortly before eating, arrange all the vegetables in a basket or bowl (lined with a cloth napkin for a nice touch) and set it on the table. Pour the olive oil and lemon juice into two separate small bowls and place in the centre of the table along with a bowl of sea salt and the pepper mill. Set both places with a plate and a small bowl, so that you and your companion can mix together oil, lemon juice, salt and pepper as the will takes you.

Step two Dip the raw vegetables into the dip, stir them around and eat!

As an alternative, offer a chilli-infused olive oil, home made, naturally. Just stuff a handful of dried chillies in a bottle and then fill up with olive oil, adding a few cloves of garlic or a sprig or two of thyme and rosemary if you like. Store it, sealed, in a dark cupboard.

Serves 2

1 carrot, cut into batons

½ fennel bulb, cut into slivers

6 radishes, preferably with their leaves, cleaned

2 celery sticks, cut into batons 10cm (4in) long

50ml (2fl oz) extra-virgin olive oil

juice of 1 lemon

sea salt and pepper

Poor Man's Asparagus

This poor man is not to be pitied, for if he can dine on leeks vinaigrette he will have plenty to savour. This is one of those simple, classic dishes that definitely adds up to more than the sum of its parts. Make it several hours in advance to allow the leeks to drink in some of the vinaigrette, and serve at room temperature.

Serves 1

4 medium leeks

1 hard-boiled egg, shelled

1 tbsp chopped fresh flat-leaf parsley

for the dressing

3 tbsp extra-virgin olive oil

1 tbsp white wine vinegar

1 garlic clove, crushed

½ tsp Dijon mustard

salt and pepper

Step one Trim the leeks and wash them thoroughly. Lay them in a wide pan with enough boiling salted water to come half way up the leeks. Bring to the boil, then cover and simmer gently until tender, turning them once – allow about 8–10 minutes. Meanwhile put all the dressing ingredients in a jam jar and shake well to mix.

Step two Drain the leeks really thoroughly; watery leeks will spoil practically any dish and this one is no exception. While they are still warm, arrange them in a serving dish and pour over the dressing. Turn them carefully until they are nicely coated. Set aside to cool down.

Step three While the leeks are cooling, mash the hard-boiled egg with a fork into tiny crumbs. Shortly before serving, scatter the leeks with the egg and parsley.

Baked Goats' Cheese with Lavender

French friends tell me that lavender and goats' cheese is all the rage in France, so I gave it a whirl. You might not expect them to be good companions but, surprisingly enough, they are. Here the goats' cheese (use the semi-soft variety with a soft, bloomy, white rind) is first marinated then baked with lavender to serve as a first course, with a salad dressed with walnut oil and lavender or balsamic vinegar.

Step one Carefully trim the rind off the bottom and top of the cheeses, then cut each one into 3 slices. To make the marinade, oil a dish large enough to take the goats' cheese slices in a single layer. Pick the lavender flowers off the spikes and scatter half of them, with half the lavender leaves, over the base of the dish. Lay the goats' cheese on top, then sprinkle over the remaining lavender flowers and leaves and season generously with freshly ground black pepper. Drizzle over the olive oil. Cover and leave to marinate for at least an hour, turning the cheeses carefully once or twice.

Step two Meanwhile, toast the bread lightly on both sides, then stamp out rounds a little larger than the goats' cheeses. To make the dressing, whisk the lavender or balsamic vinegar with the sugar, salt and pepper, then gradually whisk in the walnut oil. Taste and adjust the seasoning.

Step three Preheat the grill. Shortly before sitting down to eat, carefully extract the slices of goats' cheese from the marinade, brush off the lavender and lay each one on a round of bread. Press a fresh spike of lavender flowers gently on to each one. Grill until sizzling and melted.

Step four Meanwhile, quickly toss the salad leaves in the dressing and divide between 4 plates. Lay 2 of the discs of toasted cheese on each plate and serve at once.

Serves 4

3 small goats' cheeses (e.g. Capricorn)

8 thin slices of walnut bread or brioche

8 spikes of lavender flowers

about 75–110g (3–4oz) small salad leaves (e.g. rocket, lamb's lettuce, watercress, buckler leaf, sorrel, salad burnet, claytonia, etc.)

for the marinade

5 spikes of fresh lavender flowers

4 sprigs of fresh lavender leaves, bruised then roughly chopped

3–5 tbsp extra-virgin olive oil

freshly ground black pepper

for the dressing

½ tbsp lavender vinegar or balsamic vinegar

a pinch of sugar

2 tbsp walnut oil

salt and pepper

An Excellent Mixed Salad

In 1614 the exiled Italian Giacomo Castelvetro wrote *The Fruit, Herbs and Vegetables of Italy*, a marvellous account of the fresh horticultural produce that was eaten in Italy at that time, and which he so much missed in England. Way ahead of his time, he politely admonishes us for eating too much meat and indulging in too many sweet foods. His descriptions of the healthy, delicious ways of cooking fruit, vegetables and salads that were the norm in his homeland seem surprisingly modern as you read them today. It has taken almost 400 years for us Brits to recognize the value of what we now call the Mediterranean diet, which Castelvetro wrote about so enthusiastically and warmly. His book was finally translated into English by Gillian Riley and published in 1989, and it is well worth searching out a copy. The method here describes his perfect spring salad. Gather together as many of these leaves as you can find and dress them with a simple wine vinegar and extra-virgin olive oil vinaigrette.

young leaves, tips and shoots of herbs and salad leaves, including mint, garden cress, lemon balm, salad burnet, tarragon, borage, fennel, rocket and sorrel

flowers of watercress, rosemary, sweet violets

hearts and leaves of baby lettuce

for the dressing

salt, to taste

extra-virgin olive oil

wine vinegar

Step one Of all the salads we eat in the spring, the mixed salad is the best and most wonderful of all. Take young leaves of mint, those of garden cress, basil, lemon balm, the tips of salad burnet, tarragon, the flowers and tenderest leaves of borage, the flowers of swine cress [use watercress], the young shoots of fennel, leaves of rocket, of sorrel, rosemary flowers, some sweet violets and the tenderest leaves or the hearts of lettuce.

Step two When these precious herbs have been picked clean and washed in several waters, and dried a little with a clean linen cloth, they are dressed as usual, with oil, salt and vinegar.

Tomato Salad with Mint and Cream Dressing

Tomato and basil is the famous duo, but long before basil made it big over here, tomato and mint were getting along famously. It's a happy combination, with a particular freshness that you don't get with peppery basil. You can dress the tomatoes with a straight vinaigrette, but even nicer is this rich cream dressing.

Step one Slice the tomatoes and arrange on a plate. Season with 1–2 pinches of sugar (unless they truly are sweet, slightly tart, richly flavoured Mediterranean-style tomatoes) and a little salt and freshly ground black pepper.

Step two To make the dressing, stir the vinegar into the cream and season very lightly with salt and pepper. Drizzle over the tomatoes, then scatter with mint leaves. Serve immediately.

Serves 4

450g (1lb) ripe, luscious tomatoes

1–2 pinches of sugar, if needed

a small handful of fresh mint leaves, roughly torn

salt and freshly ground black pepper

for the dressing

2 tbsp red wine vinegar

4 tbsp single cream

Moroccan Green Pepper and Preserved Lemon Salad

When I ate this salad in Morocco it was made with grilled green peppers and preserved lemon and nothing more, and it was marvellous. The trouble with such an elemental approach in this country is that our green peppers are different; when grilled, they develop a mildly bitter flavour that can be tremendous in combination with other ingredients but is too powerful to stand more or less on its own. Unless I can get hold of the long, tapering, narrow, sweet green peppers that taste more like Moroccan ones, I prefer to soften the strong taste of ordinary green peppers with the addition of diced tomato. This trio of green, yellow and red blends in great harmony, providing a deeply savoury contrast to some of the sweeter salads of the Moroccan table though it is also good served with a herb-strewn omelette.

Serves 4

3 green peppers, grilled, skinned and seeded (see page 67)

3 ripe, well-flavoured tomatoes, seeded and finely diced

½ preserved lemon (see page 156), pulp discarded, skin finely diced

3 tbsp chopped fresh flat-leaf parsley

1 tbsp lemon juice

1½ tbsp extra-virgin olive oil

salt and freshly ground black pepper

Step one In a large bowl, mix all the ingredients, then taste and adjust the seasoning. Serve lightly chilled or at room temperature, having drained off excess dressing.

The Severnshed's Bazargan

Bazargan is a traditional Syrian dish, adopted by the Damascene Jewish community and generally associated with Friday dinners, but this version has been updated by Raviv Hadad, head chef at the Severnshed in Bristol. The surprising combination of cauliflower, bulgar (cracked wheat), nuts, spices and pomegranate molasses is inspirational.

Step one Place the bulgar in a bowl, season with salt and cover with cold water. Leave to soak for about 1 hour, until al dente (tender but still with a slight chewiness to it). Drain thoroughly, squeezing out excess water.

Step two While the bulgar is soaking, dry-fry the spices for the dressing until they begin to release their fragrance, then let them cool. Pound to a powder in a mortar, or grind in an electric spice/coffee grinder.

Step three To make the dressing, seed and finely chop the chilli (or chillies if you are using more than one). Whisk the oil with the pomegranate syrup, tomato purée, lemon juice and zest, spices and chopped chilli. The dressing will keep, covered, for 3–4 days in the fridge, so you can prepare it in advance.

Step four Mix the drained bulgar with the cauliflower, radishes, parsley, nuts and the dressing. Spoon into a serving bowl, and place on the table. Serve it as a starter, or even a vegetarian main course on a summer's day, with good bread.

Pomegranate syrup is available from some good supermarkets, usually from their specialist shelves, and from Middle Eastern groceries. Its fruity, tart flavour is tremendous in salads.

Serves 6–8

350g (12oz) bulgar

salt

1 cauliflower, broken into small florets

8 rosy red radishes, quartered

a handful of fresh flat leaf parsley, chopped

110g (4oz) hazelnuts, toasted and coarsely chopped

50g (2oz) pine nuts, toasted and coarsely chopped

150g (5oz) walnuts, toasted and coarsely chopped

for the dressing

1 tsp allspice berries

1 tsp each cumin and coriander seeds

1 red chilli (or more)

225ml (8fl oz) extra-virgin olive oil

75ml (3fl oz) pomegranate syrup

150ml (¼ pint) tomato purée

juice and finely grated zest of 1 lemon

Fried Halloumi Salad

Everyone knows the classic Greek salad, one of the best salads of the Mediterranean. Well, this is a variation on the theme, which, with its hot, salty, fried cheese, becomes a light main course in itself. The majority of the salad ingredients can be assembled (but not tossed into the dressing) an hour or two ahead, and then covered and stored in the fridge until 15 minutes before serving, but don't fry the cheese until the last minute.

Serves 4–6

1 cos lettuce

175g (6oz) cherry tomatoes, halved

12–18 Kalamata olives

1 cucumber, peeled, halved lengthways and cut in thick half moons

8 quail's eggs, boiled, shelled and halved (optional)

1 red pepper, grilled, skinned, seeded and cut into strips (see page 67)

1 green pepper, grilled, skinned, seeded and cut into strips (see page 67)

250g (9oz) halloumi or kefalotyri cheese

2 tbsp extra-virgin olive oil

for the dressing

3 tbsp extra-virgin olive oil

juice of ½ large lemon

2 tsp rigani or dried oregano

salt and freshly ground black pepper

Step one Thickly shred the cos lettuce and place it in a wide, shallow bowl. Arrange the tomatoes, olives, cucumber, quails' eggs (if using) and skinned peppers over it. Cover with cling film and keep cool for up to 2 hours. Bring back to room temperature before finishing the salad.

Step two To make the dressing, whisk the oil with the lemon juice, rigani or oregano, salt and pepper. Set aside until needed.

Step three Shortly before serving, drain the halloumi or kefalotyri and cut it into 1cm (½in) wide batons. Heat the 2 tablespoons of oil over a high heat. Fry the cheese briskly until browned on all sides and, as soon as it is done, lay it on the salad. Quickly whisk the dressing one last time and then spoon over the cheese and the salad. Toss at the table and serve quickly, while the fried cheese is still warm.

Just in case you need a reminder, a straight Greek salad is made with chunks of juicy, ripe tomato, thick, peeled cucumber crescents, thinly sliced rings of onion, sometimes with the addition of shredded cos lettuce and rings of green pepper. On top sits a fine slab of feta cheese, sprinkled with dried oregano. The whole salad is dotted with crinkly black olives, and dressed with good olive oil, wine vinegar or lemon juice, salt and pepper.

Griddled Potato, Tomato and Red Onion Salad

A delightfully fresh but hearty summer salad.

Step one Begin by mixing the sliced onions with the salt, vinegar and sugar. Leave for ½–1 hour, stirring occasionally, then squeeze the now floppy onions with your hands and place in a salad bowl. Reserve the juices.

Step two Preheat a ridged griddle. Peel the cooked potatoes and slice them about 1cm (½in) thick. When the griddle is hot, brush it lightly with a little oil. Brush each side of each potato slice with oil and griddle until striped with dark marks on either side. Alternatively, you can grill or barbecue them.

Step three Add the grilled potato slices to the onions, together with the tomatoes, mixed herbs and the juice from the onions. Mix and season with pepper, but no more salt. Just before serving, stir in the sunflower or olive oil.

Serves 4

2 red (or white) onions, thinly sliced

2 tsp salt

1½ tbsp white wine vinegar

1 tbsp caster sugar

700g (1½lb) main-crop but slightly waxy potatoes (e.g. Estima or Cara), boiled in their skins until just done

oil, for brushing

450g (1lb) tomatoes, cut into rough chunks

chopped mixed parsley, chives and mint

2–3 tbsp of sunflower or extra-virgin olive oil

pepper

Umbrian Panzanella

The best-known version of the Italian salad *panzanella* is made with juicy, scarlet, high-summer tomatoes, but several years ago, when I was working in Umbria, I came across this version without a tomato in sight but every bit as good. Both versions of the salad are made with stale bread, soaked to soften it then stirred into the salad to give substance and flavour.

Serves 4

1 thick slice of stale bread (weighing about 50g/2oz after crusts have been removed)

2 celery sticks, finely diced

2 carrots, finely diced

½ fennel bulb, finely diced

½ red onion, finely diced

4 tbsp extra-virgin olive oil

1 tbsp red wine vinegar

6–8 fresh basil leaves, roughly-torn

salt and freshly ground black pepper

Step one Tear the bread into pieces and place in a bowl. Sprinkle fairly generously with water and leave to soften for 5–10 minutes.

Step two Squeeze excess water from the bread with your hands, mushing the bread up as you do so. Place the bread into a large bowl and stir in all the remaining ingredients. Cover and leave at room temperature for an hour or so. Stir well before serving.

Ensure that you use good-quality bread (sliced white will not do): the more flavour it has, the better. Last time I made it I used a stale loaf of shop-bought wholemeal, which worked very well.

Red Cabbage, Orange and Black Olive Salad

I love that Germanic way of slowly cooking red cabbage with apple, spices, vinegar and sugar for several hours until it has reduced down to a glorious, purple, sweet–sour mass but, wonderful though that is, it's not the only way to deal with red cabbage. Swiftly stir-fried, it develops a fresh-tasting, half-soft, half-crisp texture that is enormously satisfying. You can season it Chinese style, with plenty of garlic, spring onions, ginger and maybe a few shakes of soy sauce, and serve it hot, but stir-frying is also an excellent way of taking the rather insistently cabbagey, chewy edge off the raw vegetable for a lively salad. That's what I've done here and, to give colour and zip, I've added fresh pieces of orange and salty black olives.

Step one Cut the tough core out of the cabbage and slice the rest very thinly. Heat the oil in a wok over a very high heat indeed. Add the cabbage and onion and stir-fry briskly, without reducing the heat, until it is soft and floppy but still has a slight crunch – about 5–6 minutes.

Step two Turn off the heat, add the lemon juice, Worcestershire sauce, sugar, salt and pepper and toss together. Let the mixture cool until tepid, then mix in the orange and black olives. Taste and adjust the seasoning. Serve at room temperature.

It really is a false economy to buy cheap stoned olives. They tend to taste soapy and rather unpleasant, and they don't keep as long as olives with their stones in.

Serves 4

½ red cabbage
3 tbsp extra-virgin
olive oil
1 onion, thinly sliced
juice of ½ lemon
1 tsp Worcestershire
sauce
a pinch of sugar
1 orange, peeled and
thinly sliced
12 black olives
salt and freshly ground
black pepper

Roasted Carrot Salad

This is an old favourite of ours, but if you have never tasted roasted carrots it will come as something of a revelation. The dry heat of the oven intensifies their flavour, making them irresistibly delicious. Tossed with lemon juice, garlic and mint, then left to cool, they are sensationally good.

Serves 4

900g (2lb) large
carrots, peeled

4 tbsp extra-virgin
olive oil

½ tsp coarse salt

2 small garlic cloves,
finely chopped

juice of ½ large lemon

a handful of fresh mint
leaves, roughly torn

freshly ground black
pepper

Step one Preheat the oven to 200°C/400°F/gas 6. Cut the carrots into 7.5cm (3in) lengths. Halve the lower ends lengthways and cut the fatter upper ends into quarters lengthways. Put the carrots into a roasting tin or ovenproof dish with the oil and salt. Turn the carrots to coat them evenly. Roast for about 45 minutes, turning occasionally, until very tender and patched with brown.

Step two Tip the contents of the pan into a shallow serving dish and add all the remaining ingredients. Taste and add a little more salt if needed. Leave to cool to room temperature before serving.

For a video masterclass on chopping vegetables, go to
www.mykitchentable.co.uk/videos/choppingvegetables

KITCHEN
TABLE

Carrot and Raisin Salad

This is a straightforward grated carrot salad, dressed with a light vinaigrette and enlivened with a few raisins. It is great served with Spinach and Feta Pie (see page 111).

Step one In a bowl, mix the grated carrots with the raisins. In a smaller bowl, whisk the vinegar or lemon juice with the mustard, salt and pepper, then gradually whisk in the oil. Pour over the carrots and raisins and turn to mix.

Try adding a sprinkling of pumpkin or sunflower seeds as well.

Serves 4–6

3 large carrots (about
275g/10oz), peeled
and grated

25g (1oz) raisins

2 tsp white wine
vinegar or lemon juice

½ tsp Dijon mustard

2 tbsp sunflower or
extra-virgin olive oil

salt and freshly ground
black pepper

Beetroot, Potato, Apple and Chive Salad

A salad of home-cooked beetroot (always so much nicer than the ready-cooked stuff), dressed with a mustardy vinaigrette and sprinkled copiously with chopped chives, makes a perfect first course with hunks of good bread to mop up the scarlet juices. This is a more substantial salad, with potato and sweet nuggets of apple, too, dressed with mayonnaise or soured cream. More complicated it may be, but the chives still play an important role in seasoning the combination of flavours and textures.

Serves 4–6

310–350g (11–12oz) raw beetroot

1 crisp apple

lemon juice

250g (9oz) new potatoes or waxy salad potatoes, cooked in their skins and sliced

3 tbsp snipped fresh chives, plus a few extra to garnish

4 tbsp mayonnaise (or 4 tbsp soured cream mixed with ½ tbsp tarragon vinegar or white wine vinegar)

salt and freshly ground black pepper

Step one Preheat the oven to 160°C/325°F/gas 3. To cook the beetroot, trim the stalks about 2.5cm (1in) away from the beetroot itself. Do not cut off the long tapering root. Wash the beetroot clean as necessary, trying not to pierce the skin. Wrap each beetroot separately in silver foil. Place in a roasting tin and roast in the oven for about 1½–2 hours, depending on the size of the beetroot, until the skin scrapes easily away from the root end of one of the largest spheres. Cool slightly, then peel and cut into 1cm (½in) chunks.

Step two Quarter and core the apple (but do not peel), then dice and toss in a little lemon juice to prevent browning. In a large bowl, mix together the apple, beetroot, potatoes, 3 tablespoons snipped chives, mayonnaise (or soured cream and vinegar), salt and pepper. Taste and adjust the seasoning, then sprinkle with the remaining snipped chives. Serve at room temperature.

Fattoush

Fattoush is a Middle Eastern salad, an orchestra of ingredients that come together in a carefully thought-out harmony. One of the players should, by rights, be fleshy-lobed purslane. Its astringency is balanced by all the other bits and bobs but it adds a crucial note to the whole. If purslane is quite out of the question, the salad will still be enormously enjoyable, even if it is missing out ever so slightly.

Step one Spread the cucumber dice out in a colander and sprinkle lightly with salt. Leave for 30 minutes to drain, then rinse and dry on kitchen paper.

Step two Split open the pitta bread and toast with the opened side to the heat until browned and crisp. Break up into small pieces and place in a salad bowl. Sprinkle with about a third of the lemon juice.

Step three Add all the remaining ingredients, including the cucumber. Turn with your hands to mix. Taste and adjust the seasoning, adding more lemon juice if needed.

Serves 6–8

1 cucumber, diced

1 pitta bread

juice of 1 lemon

4 tomatoes, deseeded and diced

6 spring onions or 1 red onion, chopped

leaves of a small bunch of fresh purslane, chopped if large

4 tbsp chopped fresh flat-leaf parsley

2 tbsp chopped fresh mint

2 tbsp chopped fresh coriander

2 garlic cloves, crushed

6–7 tbsp extra-virgin olive oil

salt and freshly ground black pepper

Carrot and Watercress Salad

This recipe, given to me by Manisha Gambhir Harkins, was what clinched my newfound love of curry leaves. She often ate this salad as a child – it is very common in southern India, served usually in small quantities as part of a *thali*, alongside another salad and more substantial dishes. The American in her has added the watercress, and she now often serves it as a starter before a rich meal. It is addictively good, with a marvellous vivid, fresh taste that leaves you feeling incredibly healthy.

Serves 2–3

3 small or 2 medium carrots, grated

a good handful of watercress, trimmed of tougher stems

a pinch of salt

1½–2 tbsp groundnut or sunflower oil

a small handful of curry leaves, preferably fresh, though dried will do

1 tsp black mustard seeds

½ tsp cumin seeds

a couple of squeezes of lime juice (optional)

Step one Mix the carrots, watercress and salt together in a small heatproof bowl.

Step two Heat the oil in a small pan or a wok. Add the curry leaves and mustard seeds. As soon as the mustard seeds begin to pop, draw the pan off the heat and add the cumin seeds. Return the pan to the heat, cover, and let the seeds pop for about 10 more seconds. Draw off the heat and pour straight over the salad. Add the lime juice, if using, then mix well and serve.

Middle Eastern Herb Salad with Bulgar, Saffron and Chickpeas

This heavily herb-strewn salad is a more substantial version of the Middle Eastern tabbouleh, fleshed out with chickpeas. The bulgar forms a relatively minor part – it is the herbs themselves, lots and lots of them, that take pride of place.

Step one Put the bulgar or couscous into a bowl with the saffron and pour over the water. Stir, then leave for 20–30 minutes to swell and soften. Meanwhile, pick the leaves from the bunches of parsley, mint and coriander and chop them finely.

Step two Drain off any water that has not been absorbed by the bulgar or couscous. Add all the remaining ingredients to the bowl, stir together, then cover and refrigerate for a few hours or, better still, overnight, to allow the flavours to mellow and blend and the leaves to soften. Stir again, then taste and adjust the seasoning. Serve as a first course with good bread, or as an accompaniment.

Although this salad tastes just fine as soon as it is made, it improves vastly if left for a good few hours or, preferably, overnight.

Serves 8

50g (2oz) bulgar or couscous

a large pinch of saffron strands

150ml (¼ pint) boiling water

1 bunch of fresh flat-leaf parsley

1 small bunch of fresh mint

1 small bunch of fresh coriander

200g (7oz) dried chickpeas, soaked overnight and cooked, or a 400g (14oz) tin of chickpeas, well drained

finely grated zest and juice of 1 lemon

½ red chilli, seeded and finely chopped

250g (8oz) tomatoes, seeded and finely diced

1 tsp ground cinnamon

8 tbsp extra-virgin olive oil

2 garlic cloves, crushed

salt and freshly ground black pepper

Beetroot, Orange and Walnut Salad

This, I admit, is a salad that has elicited a mixed response. I love the combination of beetroot and orange with scented orange-flower water, but several of my friends don't. 'Too bad', I say, but then I soften and concede that you could leave the orange-flower water out, and you would still have an excellent salad to put on the table. I leave the decision in your hands.

Serves 4–6

500g (1lb 2oz) cooked fresh beetroot, skinned and cut into 1cm (½in) cubes, preferably while still warm

2 oranges, peeled and sliced

25g (1oz) walnut halves, lightly toasted, to garnish

for the dressing

3 tbsp lemon juice

2 tsp orange-flower water (optional)

¼ tsp ground cumin

1 tbsp extra-virgin olive oil

1 tbsp caster sugar

salt and freshly ground black pepper

Step one Place the cubed beetroot in a bowl. Mix together all the dressing ingredients. Reserve 1 tablespoon of this dressing and spoon the rest over the beetroot. Leave to marinate for at least 1 hour, then taste and adjust the seasoning.

Step two Just before serving, arrange the orange slices in a circle on a plate and drizzle the reserved dressing over them. Drain excess dressing from the beetroot and then pile it in the centre of the oranges. Garnish with the walnut halves, and serve.

Moroccan Cooked Tomato and Green Pepper Salad

This 'salad' belongs, really, in the family of Mediterranean vegetable and tomato stews, along with the Provençal ratatouille, and Mallorcan tumbet (see pages 95 and 100). However, it relies on green peppers and tomatoes alone, and is so thick that you can spread it on bread. Serve it as a first course, on its own, with warm bread to scoop it up, or as part of a collection of small salads, both cooked and uncooked.

Step one Preheat the grill and, when hot, grill the green peppers close to the grill, turning them frequently until they are blackened and blistered all over. Drop them into a plastic bag and knot or seal. Leave until cool enough to handle, then pull off the skins. Remove the stem and seeds and then cut the flesh into strips. Cut the strips more or less into thirds. Reserve.

Step two Heat the olive oil in a frying pan and add the tomatoes, tomato purée, sugar and garlic. Cook for about 10 minutes, stirring and mashing the tomatoes down until they form a sauce. Now add the peppers, paprika, cumin, salt and a pinch of cayenne pepper (or a couple of pinches if you fancy a definite tingle of heat). Continue cooking, stirring frequently, until all the watery juices have evaporated and the mixture is starting to fry again in the oil – about 15 minutes, depending on the temperature.

Step three Taste and adjust the seasoning and then turn the mixture into a bowl or onto a shallow plate and leave to cool. Serve at room temperature, garnished, if you wish, with a sprig or two of parsley.

Serves 4

4 green peppers
2 tbsp extra-virgin olive oil
800g (2lb) ripe, red tomatoes, skinned, seeded and chopped
1 tbsp tomato purée
1 tsp caster sugar
3 garlic cloves, chopped
1 tsp sweet paprika
1½ tsp ground cumin
salt and cayenne pepper
1–2 fresh parsley sprigs, to garnish (optional)

White Cabbage Salad

We ate this the very first night we arrived in Marrakech, where it was set on the table amongst a bevy of other more glamorous salads. Cabbage? Rather dull, we all thought, until the moment we took our first mouthfuls. Sensational: bright and clean and invigorating. The plate was swiftly emptied, and the salad underlined in my notebook. Here, then, is a salad to conjure with, despite its apparent simplicity.

Serves 4

¼ white cabbage
1 tbsp coarse sea salt
juice of 1 lemon
2 tbsp extra-virgin olive oil
2 tbsp chopped fresh flat-leaf parsley
freshly ground black pepper

Step one Cut the tough core out of the cabbage, then shred the rest thinly. Place in a bowl with the other ingredients and mix thoroughly. Taste and adjust the seasoning, then serve lightly chilled.

Moroccan Lentil Salad

This earthy lentil salad, with its mild hints of cumin and paprika, provides a good contrast to a mixture of salads made with fresh and cooked vegetables.

Step one Put the lentils into a saucepan with the onion and garlic, and add water to cover. Bring to the boil and simmer for 15–45 minutes, depending on the age of the lentils, until just tender but not sludgy. Drain thoroughly and discard the pieces of onion and the garlic.

Step two Mix together all the remaining ingredients and pour over the lentils while still hot. Stir to combine and leave to cool. Serve at room temperature.

Serves 4

200g (7oz) brown or green lentils

1 onion, quartered

3 garlic cloves, peeled but left whole

2 tbsp chopped fresh flat leaf parsley

2 tbsp lemon juice

1 tsp ground cumin

1 tsp sweet paprika

a hint of harissa

5 tbsp extra-virgin olive oil

salt

Grilled Aubergine Salad

A favourite salad of mine – a dark gleaming mass of aubergines, smoky and rich with a garlicky hiss. Grilled aubergine slices, simply salted, then brushed with oil and seasoned before grilling, are good hot, too.

Serves 6

2 large aubergines

salt

2–3 tbsp chopped fresh mixed herbs, including flat-leaf parsley, basil and/or chives

for the dressing

1½ tbsp white or red wine vinegar

1–2 cloves garlic, peeled and crushed

7 tbsp extra-virgin olive oil

salt and freshly ground black pepper

Step one To make the dressing, mix the vinegar with the garlic, pepper and a little salt. Whisk in the olive oil a tablespoonful at a time.

Step two Slice the aubergine into 1cm (½in) thick discs. Sprinkle lightly with salt and leave for 30 minutes to 1 hour. Wipe dry with kitchen paper. Toss with half the dressing. Grill, close to the heat, until browned on both sides. Toss with enough of the remaining dressing to moisten, then leave to cool. Toss with the chopped herbs and serve.

KITCHEN TABLE

Have you made this recipe? Tell us what you think at
www.mykitchentable.co.uk/blog

72

Pumpkin, Sweetcorn and Sweet Potato Stew

This is a substantial stew, full of the orange and yellow hues of autumn.

Step one Preheat the oven to 180°C/350°F/gas 4. Cut a lid off the top of the pumpkin. Scoop out the seeds then excavate at least 450–700g (1–1½lb) of the flesh. Chop it roughly and reserve.

Step two Dry-fry the coriander and cumin seeds in a heavy pan over a medium heat for a couple of minutes. When they are beginning to scent the room, snap the dried chilli into 2 or 3 pieces and add it to the spices along with the oregano. Dry-fry for a further 30 seconds or so, shaking the pan constantly. Tip into a cold bowl, let cool, then grind to a fine powder. Reserve.

Step three Peel and chop the onions and garlic and fry them in the oil in a very large casserole or saucepan (I use my preserving pan), without letting them brown. When they are tender, add the spices and stir about for a minute. Now add the tinned tomatoes, tomato purée, Worcestershire sauce, a small shake of Tabasco, the apple juice and 600ml (1 pint) water. Bring to the boil and simmer for 10 minutes.

Step four Cut all the peeled potatoes into 2.5cm (1in) cubes and add them, along with the pumpkin flesh, to the saucepan. Simmer for a further 20–30 minutes, until the pumpkin has dissolved to thicken the juices and the potatoes are almost tender. Meanwhile, peel and seed the marrow and cut it into 2.5cm (1in) cubes. Add it to the stew, along with the prunes, sweetcorn and coconut milk. Stir in well, then leave to simmer for a further 15 minutes. Taste and adjust the seasoning, adding more Tabasco if you like. Scatter over a little fresh coriander, and then scatter a little more over each bowl as you serve.

Serves 8–10

1 large pumpkin
1 tbsp coriander seeds
1½ tbsp cumin seeds
1 dried red chilli
1 tbsp dried oregano
2 large onions
5 garlic cloves
3 tbsp sunflower oil
400g (14oz) tin of chopped tomatoes, with their juice
1 tbsp tomato purée
1 tbsp Worcestershire sauce
Tabasco sauce, to taste
300ml (½ pint) apple juice
700g (1½lb) each sweet and regular potatoes, peeled
1 small marrow
30 prunes
350g (12oz) frozen sweetcorn, thawed
400ml (14fl oz) coconut milk
4 tbsp chopped fresh coriander
salt and freshly ground black pepper

I prefer to use prunes with the stone in for this stew. This dish can be made in advance and reheated when needed.

Tatin of Caramelized Onions and Garlic with Goats' Cheese Pastry

The natural sweetness of onions and garlic is emphasized here by gently caramelizing them but the pastry counters it with the salty weight of goats' cheese. It's easy to make, with a touch of drama built in at the end as the pan is inverted to reveal the finished tart in its full, glossy glory.

Serves 4

50g (2oz) unsalted butter

3 onions, sliced

10 garlic cloves, peeled, blanched for 2 minutes in boiling salted water, then drained

50g (2oz) caster sugar

1½ tbsp red wine vinegar

salt and freshly ground black pepper

for the pastry

175g (6oz) plain flour

¼ tsp salt

75g (3oz) softened butter

75g (3oz) rinded goats' cheese, crumbled

1 tsp fresh thyme leaves

Step one To make the pastry, sift the flour and salt into a bowl. In another bowl, beat the butter and goats' cheese together vigorously until well mixed and softened, then work in the thyme leaves and the sifted flour. Gather up into a ball, knead briefly to smooth out, then wrap in clingfilm. Chill for at least 30 minutes.

Step two Find a heavy-based ovenproof frying pan or cake tin about 25cm (10in) in diameter. Roll the pastry out into a rough circle a tad larger than the pan or tin. Slide the pastry onto a baking sheet or large plate, cover loosely and return to the fridge until needed. Preheat the oven to 190°C/375°F/gas 5.

Step three Melt the butter in the frying pan or tin. Add the onions and prepared garlic. Fry gently for 5–7 minutes, until the onions are tender and the garlic starting to soften. Sprinkle over the sugar, vinegar, a touch of salt and plenty of freshly ground black pepper. Stir and continue cooking for another 10 minutes or so, until both onions and garlic are very lightly caramelized.

Step four Draw off the heat and distribute the onions and garlic evenly around the pan. Quickly lay the pastry on top, gently pressing it over the onions and garlic and tucking the edges down into the pan. Bake for 20–30 minutes, until golden brown.

Step five Take the tart out of the oven, then run a knife around the edge of the pan. Place a large plate on top and invert the tart in one swift motion. If any of the topping sticks to the pan, don't worry; scrape it off and spread it on the tarte Tatin – no one will be any the wiser. Serve at once while hot, or when just warm.

Three Allium Tart

Three alliums – Chinese chives, garlic and red onions – are all brought together in one savoury tart. If you can't get Chinese chives you can use ordinary ones, as they can just survive the slow, moist cooking in cream and eggs. I like the contrast of the rich creamy filling with the complexities of the three allied garlic–onion flavours, but if you prefer something a little lighter, replace half the cream with milk.

Step one First make the pastry. Sift the flour with the salt, then rub the butter into the flour until it resembles fine breadcrumbs. Make a well in the centre and add the egg yolk and enough iced water to form a soft dough 1½ 2 tablespoons of water should be enough. Mix quickly and lightly, and knead very briefly to smooth out. Wrap in cling film and chill for at least 30 minutes in the fridge. Bring back to room temperature before using.

Step two Preheat the oven to 190°C/375°F/gas 5. Roll the pastry out and use it to line a 23cm (9in) tart tin. Leave it to rest for a few minutes, then prick the base all over with a fork and line with foil or greaseproof paper. Weight down with baking beans, then bake blind for 10 minutes. Remove the beans and paper and return the pastry case to the oven for 5 minutes or so to dry out.

Step three Blanch the cloves of garlic in boiling water for 1 minute, then drain. Heat the cream and milk in a saucepan until simmering. Add the garlic cloves and poach gently for 10–15 minutes until very tender. Lift out with a slotted spoon into a bowl. Mash to a paste, then work in the egg yolks and egg. Whisk in the cream and milk and plenty of salt and pepper. Reduce the oven temperature to 160°C/325°F/gas 3.

Step four Sauté the onions briskly in the olive oil until tender and browned. Scoop out and drain on kitchen paper. When cool, spread out in the pastry case. Scatter over the chives and cheese, then pour over the garlic and cream mixture. Return the tart to the oven for 30–40 minutes, until just set but still with a slight wobble in the centre. Serve warm or cold as preferred.

Serves 6–8

for 350g (12oz) shortcrust pastry
225g (8oz) plain flour
a pinch of salt
100g (4oz) chilled butter, diced
1 egg yolk, beaten
iced water

for the filling
1 head of garlic, separated into cloves and peeled
225ml (8fl oz) single cream
200ml (7fl oz) milk
2 egg yolks
1 egg
2 red onions, sliced
2 tbsp extra-virgin olive oil
2 tbsp snipped fresh Chinese chives
75g (3oz) Taleggio or dolcelatte cheese, cut into cubes
salt and freshly ground black pepper

Omelette Tourangelle

A big fluffy omelette flavoured with *fines herbes* (tarragon, parsley, chervil, chives), filled with soft goats' cheese and served with a roast tomato sauce. If you can't get chervil, then substitute a small amount of dill weed, fennel leaves or sweet cicely.

Serves 2 (generously)

5 eggs

3 tbsp chopped fresh *fines herbes* (a mixture of tarragon, parsley, chervil and chives)

a generous knob of butter

50g (2oz) young soft goats' cheese or crumbled semi-soft goats' cheese, rinds removed

salt and freshly ground black pepper

for the roast tomato sauce

8 plum tomatoes, halved

3 whole garlic cloves, unpeeled

1 fresh thyme sprig

1 fresh rosemary sprig

½ tsp caster sugar

2 tbsp extra-virgin olive oil

salt and freshly ground black pepper

Step one Preheat the oven to 200°C/400°F/gas 6. To make the sauce, place the halved tomatoes cut-side up in an oiled, shallow ovenproof dish in a single layer. Tuck the garlic cloves, thyme and rosemary among them. Sprinkle with the sugar, season with salt and pepper and drizzle over the olive oil. Place in the oven and roast, uncovered, for 40–50 minutes, until the tomatoes are patched with brown.

Step two Remove the thyme and rosemary twigs, then tip the entire contents of the dish into a food processor. Process until fairly smooth, then sieve. Taste and adjust the seasoning, and reheat when needed.

Step three Beat the eggs energetically with some salt and pepper, then stir in the herbs. Heat half the butter in a wide frying pan until it foams. Pour in half the beaten egg mixture and swirl the pan to cover the base entirely. Reduce the heat and cook more gently. When the omelette is just about cooked through, but still slightly damp and runny on top, dot half the cheese down the middle. Flip the sides over to cover and slide it out of the pan on to a warm plate. Repeat with the remaining butter, eggs and cheese. Serve the omelettes with the roast tomato sauce.

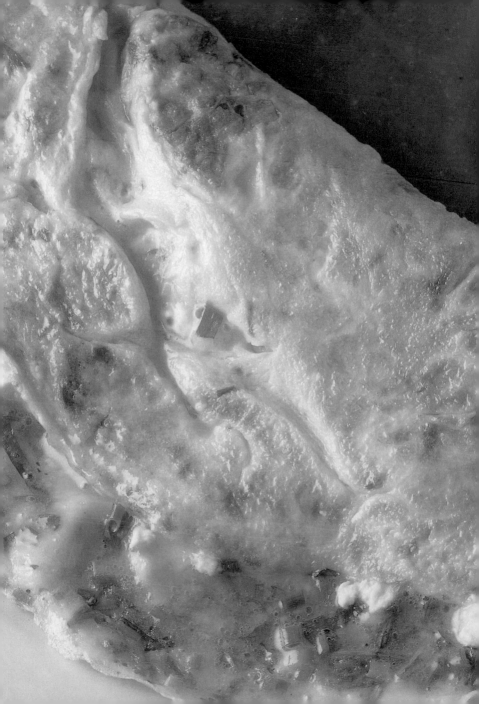

Frittata Alla Trippa (Parmesan and Parsley Omelette with Fresh Tomato Sauce)

If ever there was a name of a dish designed to confuse, this has to be it. Translated it means 'tripe omelette', from which most of us would deduce that it meant an omelette made with tripe. But it doesn't. There isn't a single shred of anything remotely tripey in it at all. Purely vegetarian, it is a homely, but excellent dish from Siena. It is, in fact, an omelette flavoured with Parmesan and parsley, then cut into strips, rather like tripe, and finished with a fresh tomato sauce – again, rather like tripe, in Italy at any rate.

Step one Whisk together the eggs, Parmesan, parsley, salt and pepper. Set aside.

Step two To make the sauce, cook the garlic in the oil for a few seconds until just beginning to brown. Add the fresh tomatoes, tomato purée, salt, pepper and about 1 teaspoon of sugar. Cook over a high heat for about 3 minutes, until lightly thickened to form a lumpy tomato sauce. Taste and adjust the seasoning. Reheat briefly when needed.

Step three Make the omelette shortly before serving. Heat the olive oil in a 28cm (11in) frying pan over a moderately high heat. Pour in the egg mixture and swirl the pan to cover the base entirely. Reduce the heat and cook more gently until the surface is just set but not dry. Carefully loosen the edges from the side of the pan, then invert on to a plate. Put the pan back on the heat, then slide the frittata back in, cooked-side up. Cook for a further minute or two just to set the underneath. Flip the sides over the middle and then turn out onto a warm serving plate.

Step four Quickly cut the frittata into ribbons about 1cm (½in) wide. Spoon over about two-thirds of the sauce (save the rest to dress vegetables or a small portion of pasta). Serve immediately as a light meal with bread and salads, or tucked into a warm roll with a smear of sauce.

Serves 1

3 large eggs

15g (½ oz) Parmesan cheese, freshly grated

1 tbsp chopped fresh flat-leaf parsley

salt and freshly ground black pepper

extra-virgin olive oil, for frying

for the tomato sauce

2 garlic cloves, chopped

2 tbsp extra-virgin olive oil

500g (1lb 2oz) fresh tomatoes, skinned, seeded and chopped

1 tbsp tomato purée

salt and freshly ground black pepper

sugar

Chak-chouka (Baked Eggs in Spiced Pepper and Tomato Stew)

This mixture of fried peppers, tomatoes and eggs flavoured with cumin comes from the southern side of the Mediterranean, from Tunisia and its neighbouring countries, where it might be served for breakfast. Back at home you may well prefer to serve it as a light main course for lunch or supper.

Serves 2–3

5 tbsp extra-virgin olive oil

2 onions, sliced

2 garlic cloves, sliced

1 small green pepper, seeded and cut into long, thin strips

1 small red pepper, seeded and cut into long, thin strips

1 heaped tsp ground cumin, plus a little extra for serving

500g (1lb 2oz) ripe tomatoes, skinned and roughly chopped

1 tbsp tomato purée

1 tsp caster sugar, if needed

6 eggs

cayenne pepper or paprika

salt and freshly ground black pepper

Step one Heat the oil in a heavy-based frying pan over a moderate heat. Add the onions, garlic and peppers and fry, stirring frequently, until soft and floppy (this will take about 10–15 minutes; don't try to hurry it). Stir in the cumin and fry for a further minute. Next, add the tomatoes, with any juice that has oozed out of them, the tomato purée, salt and pepper, and a touch of sugar if the tomatoes are very sharp. Allow the mixture to cook to a thick, but wettish, sauce. Taste and adjust the seasoning.

Step two Make a dip in the vegetable mixture with the back of a spoon, then break an egg into it. Repeat with the remaining eggs. When all the eggs are in, cover the frying pan with a lid or large plate and continue cooking gently for a further 8–10 minutes, until the eggs are set. Sprinkle the eggs with a little more salt and a light dusting of cumin and cayenne pepper or paprika and serve.

Parsnip, Carrot and Cauliflower Korma

This is a mild but warmly spiced curry, thickened with yoghurt and ground almonds. Serve with rice and relishes, such as mango chutney and sour lime pickles.

Step one Cut the parsnips and carrots into 1cm (½in) slices or, if they are large, dice them. Reserve them until needed. In a pan large enough to take all the ingredients, fry the chopped onion in the oil until golden brown. Stir in all the dry spices and, when well mixed, add the garlic, ginger and chilli. Stir gently for 1 minute. Stir in the yoghurt, a tablespoon at a time, then add the almonds. Cook, stirring, for 2 minutes.

Step two Stir in 300ml (½ pint) of water and some salt, then add the parsnips, carrots and cauliflower florets. Cover and simmer gently for 20–25 minutes, until the vegetables are almost done, stirring occasionally. Uncover the pan and simmer for 5 minutes or so. Taste and adjust the seasoning. Sprinkle with fresh coriander or parsley before serving.

You can adapt this curry to practically any vegetables that you have to hand, as long as you add those that take less time to cook 5–10 minutes or so after the slow-cooking root vegetables.

Serves 4

275g (10oz) parsnips
350g (12oz) carrots
1 medium onion, finely chopped
4 tbsp sunflower oil
1 tbsp ground cumin
2 tsp ground coriander
1 tsp ground cinnamon
1 tsp ground turmeric
2 garlic cloves, finely chopped
2.5cm (1in) fresh root ginger, very finely chopped
1 green chilli, seeded and very finely chopped
300ml (½ pint) Greek-style yoghurt
40g (1½ oz) ground almonds
275g (10oz) small cauliflower florets
finely chopped fresh coriander or parsley, to garnish
salt and freshly ground black pepper

Asparagus and Gruyère Quiche

This is a quiche to make at the height of the asparagus season when you've feasted your fill of plainly cooked asparagus. It is an excellent way of stretching a small quantity of asparagus.

Serves 6–8

1 quantity shortcrust
pastry (see page 79)

350g (12oz) asparagus

salt

110g (4oz) Gruyère
cheese

3 shallots or 1 small
onion, chopped

15g (½ oz) butter

3 eggs

150ml (¼ pint) milk

75ml (3fl oz) double
cream

1 tbsp chopped fresh
chervil or flat-leaf
parsley

salt and freshly ground
black pepper

Step one Preheat the oven to 200°C/400°F/gas 6. Line a 23cm (9in) tart tin with the pastry. Leave it to rest in the fridge for 30 minutes.

Step two Prick the base of the tart with a fork and line with greaseproof paper or foil and weight down with baking beans. Bake for 10 minutes. Remove the paper or foil and beans and return to the oven for 5 minutes to dry out. Leave to cool. Reduce the oven temperature to 180°C/350°F/gas 4.

Step three Trim the asparagus, breaking off the tough ends (save these and their cooking water for making soup). Cut into 2cm (¾in) lengths, keeping the tips separate. Pour 4cm (1½in) of water into a large pan, add salt and bring to the boil. Add the stem pieces of asparagus and simmer for 5 minutes. Add the tips and simmer gently for 2–3 minutes, until almost al dente, but still firm, then drain. If prepared in advance, cool and cover.

Step four Dice 75g (3oz) of the Gruyère and grate the remainder. Fry the shallots or onion gently in the butter until tender, without browning. Scatter the asparagus, diced Gruyère and shallots over the base of the pastry case.

Step five Whisk the eggs lightly, then whisk in the milk, cream, chervil or parsley and salt and pepper. Pour over the asparagus and cheese. Scatter the grated Gruyère over the top and bake for 25–30 minutes, until just set in the centre and nicely browned. Serve hot, warm or cold.

Pea, Ricotta and Herb Quiche

This is an enchantingly pretty, countryish quiche, with herb-flecked ricotta and peas. I think the yeast pastry is what makes this quiche extra special, but if you are pushed for time, line the tart tin with shortcrust pastry (see page 79) and bake blind before filling. Use at least three sweet, fresh herbs, such as parsley, chives, chervil, basil or marjoram. Thyme, lovage or salad burnet are good too, but use in small quantities as they are strongly flavoured. Like most quiches, this one is nicest when served warm.

Step one First make the pastry. Sift the flour with the salt, then stir in the yeast. Make a well in the centre and break in the egg. Add the oil and gradually work into the flour, adding enough water to form a soft dough. Gather the dough up into a ball, knead for 5–10 minutes until smooth and elastic, set in a clean bowl, cover and leave for about an hour in a warm place to rise until it has doubled in size.

Step two Preheat the oven to 190°C/375°F/gas 5 and prepare the filling. Beat the ricotta with the eggs, and gradually mix in the milk. Stir in 3 tablespoons of the Parmesan and all the spring onions and herbs. Season with salt and pepper.

Step three Place an upturned baking tray in the oven. Punch down the dough and knead again briefly. Using the heel of your hand, press the dough into an oiled 25cm (10in) tart tin, easing the dough to cover the base and come up around the sides. The dough should be thickest around the sides, rising up a little above the rim of the tin.

Step four Scatter the peas evenly over the dough. Stir the ricotta mixture and pour over the peas. Sprinkle the remaining tablespoon of Parmesan over the surface. Set on the hot baking tray in the oven (which gives the base of the tart an instant blast of heat) and bake for 30–35 minutes, until barely set and golden. Serve hot, warm or cold.

Serves 6–8

225g (8oz) ricotta

2 eggs

200ml (7fl oz) milk

4 tbsp freshly grated Parmesan

4 spring onions, thinly sliced

3 tbsp chopped fresh mixed sweet herbs (e.g. parsley, chives, chervil, basil, marjoram, oregano, thyme, lovage, salad burnet)

350g (12oz) cooked peas

salt and freshly ground black pepper

for the pastry

200g (7oz) strong white bread flour

salt

½ x 7g sachet easy-blend dried yeast

1 egg

3 tbsp extra-virgin olive oil, plus extra for greasing

Couscous with Roast Tomatoes, Peppers and Goats' Cheese

This is a distinctly modern, European way of using couscous, topped with an unctuous, deeply flavoured sauce made from roasted tomatoes and peppers and finished with chunks of roasted onion, pepper and tomatoes and salty goats' cheese. I cannot claim the idea as my own, sadly, since I modelled it on a recipe I saw in a press release for an Italian product, reworking it to do without the poor product in question. Apologies to the public relations company and the producers and thanks for a great idea.

Serves 4

8 plum tomatoes

1 red onion, quartered

2 red peppers, seeded and cut into chunks

1 fresh red chilli

4 garlic cloves

2 fresh thyme sprigs

3 tbsp extra-virgin olive oil

1 tbsp sherry vinegar

1 tbsp caster sugar

salt and freshly ground black pepper

for the couscous

310g (11oz) couscous

600ml (1 pint) hot chicken or vegetable stock (see page 7)

2 tbsp extra-virgin olive oil

3 tbsp chopped fresh flat-leaf parsley

110g (4oz) goats' cheese, rind removed, roughly diced

6 fresh basil leaves, shredded

Step one Preheat the oven to 220°C/425°F/gas 7. Oil a large, shallow, ovenproof dish or roasting tin. Halve the plum tomatoes and place them in it in a single layer, cut-side up, along with the onion quarters, peppers, chilli and garlic. Tuck the thyme sprigs amongst them. Drizzle over the olive oil and vinegar, then sprinkle on the sugar, salt and pepper. Roast, uncovered, for 40–45 minutes, until the onions are starting to brown at the edges.

Step two Meanwhile, put the couscous into a bowl and pour on the steaming hot stock. Leave for 15 minutes, until all the liquid has been absorbed, stirring once or twice. Drizzle over the olive oil and mix well. Cover with foil and keep warm in the oven.

Step three When the vegetables are done, pick out about half the tomatoes, peppers and onions and keep warm. Unless you want a hot sauce, remove the chilli. Tip the rest into a food processor, scraping in any juices and caramelized brown goo. Don't worry about the garlic skins. Process until smooth, then rub through a sieve. Thin with a little water or stock if necessary. Taste and adjust the seasoning.

Step four Take the couscous out of the oven, uncover, add the parsley and fork up a little to mix it in and separate the grains. Pile up in a serving dish. Pour over the sauce, arrange the reserved vegetables on top and scatter with goats' cheese and shredded basil. Serve hot.

Ratatouille

When ratatouille is good, it is very, very good, but when it's bad, it's awful. There's no point trying to make ratatouille in a smaller quantity than this. And why should you? It keeps well in the fridge for a couple of days, and tastes even better cold than hot. Never rush the cooking process; allow plenty of time for the dish to mellow to a Provençal richness.

Step one Cut the aubergine into 2.5cm (1in) chunks and the courgettes into 1cm (½in) thick slices. Place the chunks and slices in a colander and sprinkle with the salt. Leave for 30 minutes to drain, then rinse and pat dry on kitchen paper.

Step two In a wide frying pan or saucepan, cook the onion and garlic gently in the oil until tender, without browning. Add the aubergine and peppers, stir, then cover and cook for 10 minutes, stirring once or twice.

Step three Now add the courgettes, tomatoes, tomato purée, sugar, salt and pepper. Bring to the boil, then lower the heat and simmer gently, uncovered, for about 30 minutes, stirring occasionally to prevent burning.

Step four Stir in the crushed coriander seeds and continue cooking for another 10 minutes or so until all traces of wateriness have gone and the ratatouille is thick and rich. Taste and adjust seasonings, adding a little more sugar if it is on the sharp side. Serve hot or cold sprinkled with the basil or parsley and maybe a drizzle of extra-virgin olive oil.

There are different theories about how to make the perfect ratatouille. Some insist on cooking all the vegetables separately, combining them only for the last few minutes. They keep their shape better that way, but I prefer the other more standard approach. I always cook them together, adding them in stages, so that the flavours all intermingle. The key to making a good ratatouille is to allow it to burble slowly on top of the stove.

Serves 6–8

1 large aubergine

450g (1lb) courgettes,

½ tbsp salt

1 large onion, chopped

2 garlic cloves, peeled and chopped

4 tbsp extra-virgin olive oil, plus a little more for drizzling (optional)

1 green pepper, seeded and cut into 1cm (½in) wide strips

1 red pepper, seeded and cut into 1cm (½in) wide strips

1 x 400g (14oz) tin chopped tomatoes or 450g (1lb) fresh tomatoes, skinned and roughly chopped

1 tbsp tomato purée

½ tsp sugar

½ tsp coriander seeds, crushed

2 tbsp chopped fresh basil or fresh flat-leaf parsley, to garnish

salt and freshly ground black pepper

Root Vegetable Pie

This sturdy root vegetable pie wrapped in puff pastry makes a magnificent main course without breaking the bank. It's one of those recipes that somehow seems to exceed the sum of its parts, tasting ten times better than you might expect. As long as you drain the vegetables thoroughly, the pie can be constructed a couple of hours in advance, and whipped into the oven an hour or so before you plan to eat.

Serves 4–6

450g (1lb) carrots, peeled and sliced

450g (1lb) potatoes, peeled and sliced

225g (8oz) turnips, peeled and sliced

50g (2oz) butter, plus extra for greasing

450g (1lb) puff pastry, thawed if frozen

flour, for rolling out

2 tbsp finely chopped fresh flat-leaf parsley

2 tsp caraway seeds

1 egg, beaten

salt and freshly ground black pepper

Step one Bring a large pan of lightly salted water to the boil. Cook the carrot slices for about 6 minutes, then scoop out and drain. Repeat with the potatoes and turnips, keeping each vegetable separate.

Step two Butter a 5cm (2in) deep and 20cm (8in) diameter loose-bottomed cake tin. Roll out two-thirds of the pastry on a lightly floured board to give a rough circle about 33cm (13in) in diameter. Loosely fold in half and then in quarters, then lift into the tin with the centre tip of the pastry at the centre of the tin. Carefully unfold, then lift the edges and gently push the pastry down to line the sides of the tin using a small knob of pastry rolled into a ball to ease it right into the corner.

Step three Layer the potatoes, carrots, and turnips in the tin, sprinkling parsley, caraway seeds, salt and pepper between layers and dotting with butter as you go. Roll out the remaining pastry, and lay over the pie. Trim off the excess and press the edges of the pastry together firmly. Make a hole in the centre, then let the pie rest for 30 minutes in the fridge. Meanwhile, preheat the oven to 220°C/425°F/gas 7.

Step four Brush the top of the pie with beaten egg and bake for 10 minutes until golden brown. Reduce the oven temperature to 180°C/350°F/gas 4 and cook for a further 50–60 minutes. Test with a skewer to check that the vegetables are cooked and tender. Unmould carefully and serve hot or warm.

Roast Roots and Alliums with Tamarind

Roasting vegetables brings out all that is best in them, intensifying their natural flavours and caramelizing their sugar to a wonderful degree. All I've done here is add the fruity tartness of tamarind (available in blocks from Asian shops, which is much cheaper than buying the ready-made liquid now sold in some supermarkets) and spiced the roots and alliums (onions and garlic) with a touch of golden turmeric, cumin seeds and the nutty, coal-black seeds of black onion, also known as *kalonji* or nigella.

Step one Preheat the oven to 220°C/425°F/gas 7. Put the tamarind into a bowl and pour over the boiling water. Leave to soak for about 20 minutes, mashing the tamarind pulp down with a fork every now and then. Give it one final squish, and mash and mix, then rub the liquid through a sieve, pressing through as much of the soft tamarind pulp as will be parted from the seeds and fibres. Stir the tamarind liquid.

Step two Put all the ingredients, including the tamarind liquid, into a roasting tin. Turn the vegetables to coat them in the oil and tamarind mixture. Cover with foil and cook in the oven for 20 minutes. Remove the foil, give the vegetable a good stir, then return to the oven and roast for a further 45–50 minutes, stirring once or twice, until they are all very tender and patched with brown. Serve hot or warm.

Serves 6

25g (1oz) tamarind

150ml (¼ pint) boiling water

6 carrots, halved lengthways

12 small new potatoes

3 large parsnips, quartered lengthways and cored

3 red onions, quartered

1 head of garlic, divided into cloves but not peeled

4 tbsp sunflower oil

½ tsp ground turmeric

2 tsp cumin seeds

1 tsp black onion seeds

coarse sea salt and lots of freshly ground black pepper

Tumbet (Mallorcan Vegetable Stew)

Tumbet is often described as a Mallorcan version of ratatouille, but it also includes potatoes, and all the vegetables are cooked separately, before the final layering up of the ingredients. The end result is a substantial and delicious vegetable dish that can be served as a first course, side dish or main course, hot, warm or cold. Mallorcan aubergines are considered by far the best aubergines grown in Spain. Those we buy here, most of them hailing from Holland, really cannot compare in flavour. This, though, is a good way of bringing out the best in them.

Serves 4–6

1 large aubergine, sliced into discs

extra-virgin olive oil, for frying

450g (1lb) slightly waxy potatoes, e.g. Cara, sliced into discs about 5mm (¼ in) thick

2 green peppers, seeded and sliced

1 red pepper, seeded and sliced

3 garlic cloves, chopped

2 x 400g (14oz) tins chopped tomatoes

3 fresh thyme sprigs

salt and freshly ground black pepper

Step one Spread the aubergine discs out on a tray and sprinkle lightly with salt. Leave for 45–60 minutes, then rinse and pat dry.

Step two Preheat the oven to 180°C/350°F/gas 4. Fry the aubergine slices in olive oil until browned and tender. Drain on kitchen paper. Next, fry the potato slices in more olive oil, until lightly browned and just tender. Finally, fry the peppers in yet more olive oil, until limp. Drain on kitchen paper.

Step three Fry the garlic in 2 tablespoons of oil until it begins to colour. Add the tomatoes, thyme, salt and pepper and cook briskly, stirring, for about 5 minutes, until you have a thick sauce. Taste and adjust the seasoning.

Step four Layer the potatoes, aubergines and peppers in an ovenproof dish, spreading a little of the tomato sauce between each layer and seasoning with extra salt and pepper. Spoon the remaining tomato sauce over the top. Cover and bake for 30 minutes. Serve hot, warm or cold.

If you want to cut down on the oil, you could grill the aubergine (brush lightly with oil first) and peppers, or steam them both. I would be loath, however, to suggest that the potatoes should be steamed as well. The fried potatoes have a particular flavour and by dispensing with that, you would, I think, lose all traces of the original.

Yemista (Greek Stuffed Vegetables)

Vegetables make such good containers for a mixture of rice and minced lamb, or just a simple rice and herb filling.

Step one Halve the courgettes lengthways then scoop out their insides, leaving a sturdy wall of courgette to carry the stuffing. Dice the flesh and reserve. Blanch the scooped-out courgette shells in boiling, salted water for 1–2 minutes, then drain.

Step two Cut a lid off the top of each pepper and remove the seeds. Blanch the peppers and their lids for 2 minutes, as above.

Step three Cut a lid off the top of each tomato and scoop out the soft pulp inside. Roughly chop this and reserve for the stuffing. Season the inside of the tomatoes with a little salt and turn upside down on a rack to drain.

Step four Preheat the oven to 190°C/375°F/gas 5. To make the stuffing, sauté the onion and the chopped courgette in the olive oil, without browning. When they are tender, add the tomato pulp and cook for a further 1–2 minutes. Next, tip in the rice, tomato purée, cinnamon, parsley, salt and pepper and 300ml (½ pint) water. Bring to the boil and then turn the heat down low. Simmer very gently, uncovered, until all the water has been absorbed and the rice is very nearly, but not quite, cooked. Stir in the mint, pine nuts and raisins, currants or feta, if using. Taste and adjust the seasoning, ensuring it is fairly strong and punchy.

Step five Fill the vegetables loosely with the rice mixture and arrange them in a close fitting, oiled baking dish. Pop the lids back on the tomatoes and peppers and sprinkle the courgettes with breadcrumbs. Drizzle over 4 tablespoons of oil and gently pour the stock or water around the sides. Bake for 40–60 minutes, basting occasionally with the juices, until the vegetables are all very tender. Serve warm, or at room temperature.

Serves 4
3 medium courgettes
2 green peppers
2 red peppers
4 medium–large tomatoes
2 tbsp fine breadcrumbs
4 tbsp extra virgin olive oil
150ml (5fl oz) vegetable stock (see page 7) or water

for the stuffing
1 onion, chopped
4 tbsp extra-virgin olive oil
200g (7oz) long-grain rice
1 tbsp tomato purée
1 tsp ground cinnamon
4 tbsp chopped fresh flat-leaf parsley
2 tbsp chopped fresh mint
75g (3oz) pine nuts, toasted
110g (4oz) raisins or currants or 110g (4oz) feta, crumbled (optional)
salt and freshly ground black pepper

Wild Garlic Bubble and Squeak

'When midst the frying Pan, in accents savage, | The Beef so surly, quarrels with the Cabbage.' So wrote Dr William Kitchiner back in 1817. In those days, bubble and squeak was made of cold roast beef, onion and cooked cabbage. Potato didn't get a look in until near the end of the century, and eventually the beef disappeared. What we think of now as classic bubble and squeak is composed largely of potatoes and cabbage. In my version, I've replaced some of the cabbage with wild garlic leaves.

Serves 4

275g (10oz) green cabbage, Savoy cabbage or kale, cored and chopped

2–3 tbsp butter

1 onion, chopped

about 50g (2oz) wild garlic leaves

salt and freshly ground black pepper

for the mash

about 600g (1lb 4oz) floury potatoes

25g (1oz) butter

2 tbsp milk

Step one Either bake the potatoes in their skins until tender or cook them in the microwave (pierce the skins with a skewer or a fork, then place, uncovered, on a plate and microwave for 8–12 minutes, until tender). Halve the potatoes and scoop out the flesh. You should have about 500g (1lb 2oz) – leftover skins could be saved for the recipe on page 28. Put the potato flesh in a saucepan and mash thoroughly while still hot. Add the butter and some salt and place over a low heat. Beat thoroughly, gradually working in the milk to give a moderately stiff mash.

Step two Meanwhile, bring a pan of salted water to the boil and add the cabbage or kale. Simmer for about 4–5 minutes, until just tender, then drain and squeeze out all the water.

Step three Shortly before serving, mix the potato with the cabbage or kale, then taste and adjust the seasoning. Heat half the butter in a wide frying pan until it foams or sizzles. Add the onion and wild garlic leaves and fry gently until the onion is tender and the garlic limp. Scrape out and mix with the potato and cabbage.

Step four Add the remaining butter to the pan, heat through, then dollop in the potato mixture, and smooth down. Fry over a moderate heat for about 8 minutes, until the underneath is browned. Carefully slide the bubble and squeak out on to a dish, then return the pan to the heat. Invert the bubble and squeak on to another plate, then slide it back into the pan. Cook until lightly browned underneath, then serve piping hot.

Goats' Cheese and Courgette Quesadilla with Avocado, Mango and Coriander Salsa

A quesadilla is a stuffed, cooked tortilla, or, in this instance, a stack of tortillas sandwiched together with an unctuous filling and baked until the outer edges of the tortillas are crisp as a wafer and the cheese is molten.

Step one To make the salsa, peel, stone and finely dice the avocado and the mango, and finely chop the shallots and coriander. Seed the chillies and finely chop the flesh. Mix all these ingredients in a bowl with the lime juice and season to taste with salt. Cover and store in the fridge until needed.

Step two Preheat the oven to 230°C/450°F/gas 8. Cut the courgettes into matchsticks. Seed the red pepper and cut it into narrow strips. Slice the shallot. To make the filling, sauté the courgettes, pepper and shallot in the oil over a brisk heat until limp and patched with brown (about 8–10 minutes). Chop the garlic, add it to the pan and sauté for a few minutes more. Draw off the heat and stir in the coriander, vinegar, salt and pepper.

Step three Lay one tortilla on a baking tray. Spread half of the vegetable mixture over it, then sprinkle over half the goats' cheese and half of the Taleggio, Fontina or Cheddar. Lay a second tortilla over it and repeat the filling. Cover with the last tortilla and press down firmly, but not too forcefully, to even out the levels. Bake in the oven for 8–12 minutes until the tortillas are crisp at the edges and the cheese has melted.

Step four Cut into wedges and serve immediately with the avocado and mango salsa.

Serves 2

3 x 18–20cm (7–8in) flour tortillas

for the filling

2 courgettes (about 360g/12oz)

1 red pepper

1 shallot

2 tbsp extra-virgin olive oil

2 garlic cloves

2 tbsp chopped coriander

½ tbsp balsamic vinegar

75g (3oz) goats' cheese, crumbled

150g (5oz) Taleggio or Fontina cheese, rinds removed then thinly sliced, or 125g (4½ oz) medium Cheddar, grated

salt and freshly ground black pepper

for the salsa

1 avocado

1 small–medium mango

2 shallots

3 tbsp chopped coriander

1–2 red chillies

juice of 1 lime

Mushrooms with Mascarpone, Lemon and Dill Sauce

This is a recipe that I came up with when I was making supper for my children one night. At first, all I was aiming for was a simple dish of mushrooms in a white sauce, but there was only enough milk left for next morning's essential parental cuppa. There was, however, the remains of a small tub of rich mascarpone lurking in the back of the fridge, along with a couple of sprigs of dill, which goes particularly well with mushrooms. In they went, and the resulting dish, with its generous amount of sauce, was highly appreciated by the lucky infants, with enough salvaged to serve on rice for our adult supper. Fortuitous serendipity.

Serves 4

½ onion, chopped

25g (1oz) butter

250g (9oz) button mushrooms, sliced

1 tbsp plain flour

2–3 tbsp mascarpone

1–2 tbsp chopped fresh dill

1 or 2 good squeezes of lemon juice

salt and freshly ground black pepper

Step one In a saucepan, fry the onion gently in half the butter, without browning, until tender. Add the mushrooms, fry for a further minute or two, then add just enough water to almost cover the mushrooms. Season, then simmer for 10 minutes.

Step two Meanwhile, mash the remaining butter thoroughly with the flour to make a *beurre manié*. Gradually add small knobs of the *beurre manié* to the mushrooms until the liquid thickens to your liking (you may need only about half of it).

Step three Stir in the mascarpone and dill and continue to cook gently for about 3 minutes, until you have a sauce of a good consistency. Stir in the lemon juice, then taste and adjust the seasoning. Serve immediately.

Spinach and Feta Pie

This is a variation on that lovely Greek concoction, spanakopita, combining salty feta cheese with cottage cheese and Parmesan, spring onions and spinach. Frozen spinach is cheaper than fresh, and in a recipe like this it works very well. Filo pastry provides the crispest of crusts, and what isn't used straight away can be frozen for another day. There's actually enough here to feed six people, but leftovers can be reheated in the oven for lunch next day, or popped into lunchboxes when no one is eating at home.

Step one Preheat the oven to 190°C/375°F/gas 5. Cover the filo pastry with a sheet of greaseproof paper, then lay a damp tea towel over that to prevent the pastry drying out.

Step two Squeeze as much excess moisture as you can from the spinach. Sauté the spring onions and garlic lightly in the butter. Mix with the cheeses, parsley and spinach, then beat in the eggs and season with salt and pepper.

Step three Find an ovenproof dish that is more or less the same size as the halved sheets of filo (or very slightly smaller). One by one, take the first five pieces of filo and brush them lightly with oil. Lay them on top of each other in the dish and spread the filling over the top. Brush the remaining 5 sheets lightly with oil and use to cover the filling. Sprinkle the poppy seeds over the filo pastry. Bake the pie for 35–45 minutes until golden brown and crisp.

Serves 6

5 large sheets filo pastry, cut in half

350g (12oz) frozen spinach, cooked and thoroughly drained

4 spring onions, finely chopped

2 garlic cloves, crushed

25g (1oz) butter

175g (6oz) cottage cheese

175g (6oz) feta, crumbled

75g (3oz) Parmesan, freshly grated

2 tbsp chopped fresh flat-leaf parsley

4 eggs, lightly beaten

sunflower oil, for brushing

1 tbsp poppy seeds

salt and freshly ground black pepper

Slow-cooked Tomato Sauce

This smooth tomato sauce is a great accompaniment to vegetables or pasta. Once made, it can be stored, covered, in the fridge for 4 days or so, or frozen.

Serves 6–10

4 tbsp extra-virgin olive oil

1 onion, chopped

1 celery stick, chopped

1 carrot, diced

1 red pepper, seeded and diced

2 garlic cloves, roughly chopped

2 x 400g (14oz) tins tomatoes

1 tbsp tomato purée

1 fresh rosemary sprig

3 tbsp chopped fresh flat-leaf parsley

1 tbsp chopped fresh marjoram

1 dried red chilli

1 tbsp red wine vinegar

1 tbsp caster sugar

¼ tsp ground cinnamon

salt and freshly ground black pepper

Step one Heat half the olive oil in a wide, deep pan. Add the onion, celery, carrot, red pepper and garlic and fry gently until the vegetables are tender, without browning.

Step two Add the tinned tomatoes, tomato purée, rosemary, parsley, marjoram, chilli, salt and pepper. Simmer together very gently, half covered, for about 1 hour, stirring occasionally, and adding a splash or two of water if the sauce threatens to burn.

Step three Fish out and discard the rosemary stem and the chilli (unless you fancy a defiantly chillied sauce), then liquidize the sauce until smooth. Return the sauce to the pan with the remaining oil, the vinegar, sugar, and cinnamon. Simmer for a further 10 minutes or so, until the sauce is thick with a deep, concentrated flavour. Serve hot or at room temperature.

Pilaf of Beetroot with Marigold Petals and Mint and Garlic Yoghurt Relish

The dark red of the beetroot coupled with the turmeric and marigold yellows transform this into one of the most vibrantly hued rice dishes you are likely to come across, echoing the rich, deep colours of Moorish art. The taste, too, is rich and vibrant: a perfect dish for a vegetarian main course.

Step one Preheat the oven to around 170°C/325°F/gas 3. Wrap each beetroot in silver foil. Place in a roasting tin and roast for 1½–2 hours, depending on their size, until the skin scrapes away easily. Cool slightly, then peel and cut into 1cm (½in) chunks.

Step two Melt the butter with the oil in a saucepan, then add the onion and fry gently, without browning, until translucent. Add the garlic, cumin seeds, cloves and cinnamon stick and fry gently for 1 minute. Add the rice and stir for a further minute, until slightly translucent. Stir in the turmeric, then add 550ml (19fl oz) water and some salt and pepper and bring to the boil. Reduce the heat to very low, cover tightly and leave to cook for 8 minutes.

Step three Put a serving dish into the oven preheated to 110°C/225°F/gas ¼. Stir the beetroot into the rice, then cover again and leave to simmer, without stirring, for 5–8 minutes, until all the liquid has been absorbed. Set aside a few of the marigold petals for garnish and stir in the remainder. Taste and adjust the seasoning. Tip into the warmed serving dish, cover with foil and leave in the oven for 10–30 minutes to dry in its own steam.

Step four Meanwhile, make the yoghurt relish. Fry the garlic in the butter until very lightly browned. Scoop out and stir into the yoghurt with the herbs and some salt to taste.

Step five Remove the pilaf from the oven, uncover and sprinkle the remaining marigold petals over just before serving, with a bowl of yoghurt relish to spoon over the top.

Serves 4

250g (9oz) beetroot, trimmed and washed

25g (1oz) butter

1 tbsp extra-virgin olive oil

1 onion, chopped

2 garlic cloves, chopped

½ tbsp cumin seeds

2 cloves

1 cinnamon stick

250g (9oz) basmati or long-grain rice, rinsed and drained in a sieve

1 level tsp ground turmeric

petals of 2–3 marigold flowers

salt and freshly ground black pepper

for the yoghurt relish

2 garlic cloves, chopped

15g (½ oz) butter

250g (9oz) Greek-style yoghurt

2 tbsp chopped fresh mint

1 tbsp snipped fresh chives (optional)

Chinese Chive, Tomato and Sweetcorn Noodles

I can never resist a big plateful of noodles, and these ones, dressed Chinese style with Chinese chives and oyster sauce (ensure you buy the special vegetarian version), are very satisfying and make an excellent meat-free meal.

Serves 3–4

400g (14oz) fresh flat or ribbon egg noodles

1 tbsp sesame oil

2 tbsp groundnut or sunflower oil

4cm (1½in) fresh root ginger, very finely chopped

1 bunch (about 25–40g/1–1½ oz) Chinese chives, cut into 1cm (½in) lengths

175g (6oz) fresh or frozen sweetcorn kernels, thawed if frozen

3 medium tomatoes, seeded and diced

4 tbsp vegetarian oyster sauce

1 tbsp soy sauce

salt and pepper

Step one Cook the noodles according to the packet instructions. Drain thoroughly and toss with ½ tablespoon of the sesame oil.

Step two Heat up a wok over a high heat until it smokes. Add the groundnut or sunflower oil, heat through, then throw in the ginger. Give it a quick stir, then add the chives and sweetcorn. Stir-fry for about 40–60 seconds, then add the tomatoes. Stir-fry for a further 30 seconds or so, then tip in the noodles. Stir and mix lightly for about 30 seconds, then spoon in the oyster sauce, soy sauce and remaining sesame oil. Toss until the sauces are mixed in evenly and the noodles are heated through. Taste and adjust the seasoning and serve immediately.

Rocket Pizza

Taleggio adds decadent creamy richness to these pizzas.

Step one Mix the flour with the salt, sugar and yeast and make a well in the centre. Add the oil and enough water to mix to a soft, slightly sticky dough. Flour your hands and gather the dough up into a ball. Knead vigorously on a lightly floured work surface for a good 8–10 minutes until smooth and elastic. Rinse the bowl out, dry, and dust with flour. Place the dough in the bowl, turn to coat lightly in the flour and then cover with a damp cloth. Leave in a warm place for about an hour, until doubled in size.

Step two Put two baking sheets in the oven and preheat it to 230°C/450°F/gas 8. To make the sauce, put all the ingredients into a saucepan and simmer for about 20 minutes until thick, stirring occasionally. Taste and adjust the seasoning, then remove and discard the herb sprigs and let the sauce cool.

Step three Punch down the dough. Gather it together and knead it again for a few minutes, then divide it in two. Using your hands and a rolling pin, stretch the first ball of dough out to form a circle 25cm (10in) across. When it is about right, use your fingers to push dough to the edges, forming a thick rim. Lay the pizza base on another well-floured flat baking sheet (or a board, or even a piece of stiff cardboard, as long as it is well floured). Smear half the tomato sauce over the pizza, leaving the rim bare. Dot with half the capers, sun-dried tomato, mozzarella and Taleggio, if using. Drizzle a thin trickle of olive oil over the top. Make a second pizza in the same way.

Step four Open the oven and carefully shake and slide the pizzas on to the hot baking sheets inside. Bake for 15–20 minutes until the edges are browned and the cheese is sizzling.

Step five Just before serving, divide the rocket between the two pizzas. Drizzle over some more olive oil, grind a little pepper over the top, and serve.

Makes 2 pizzas

for the dough

400g (14oz) strong white bread flour

2 level tsp salt

½ tsp caster sugar

1 x 7g sachet easy-blend dried yeast

2 tbsp extra-virgin olive oil

for the tomato sauce

400g (14oz) tin chopped tomatoes

2 garlic cloves, crushed

1 tbsp extra-virgin olive oil

1 bay leaf

2 fresh parsley sprigs

1 fresh thyme sprig

salt and freshly ground black pepper

for the topping

1 tbsp capers, rinsed and soaked if salted

6 sun-dried tomato halves, roughly shredded

1 ball (125g/4½ oz) buffalo-milk mozzarella, sliced

150g (5oz) Taleggio, rinded and diced (optional)

extra-virgin olive oil

75–110g (3–4oz) rocket

Fusilli al Zucotto con Rosmarino (Pasta with Pumpkin and Rosemary)

Badia a Coltibuono is set high up in the Tuscan hills, northwest of Siena. From this beautiful place come some of the finest Tuscan olive oils. You can buy the oils directly from the shop here, as well as vinegars, fabulous honey (my favourite is the chestnut flower honey with an almost burnt edge to its sweetness) and other culinary gems. The neat, modern restaurant, tucked away in the woods beside the church, serves superb local food, which is perhaps not surprising as the whole enterprise is run by food writer Lorenza de' Medici and her daughter and fellow food writer, Emanuella. When we ate there one gloriously sunny, early autumn day, they gave us an excellent dish of pasta dressed with buttery pumpkin and rosemary. This is my version of their original.

Serves 4 as a starter or 2–3 as a main course

400g (14oz) fusilli

4 small fresh rosemary sprigs, to garnish (optional)

freshly grated Parmesan, to serve

for the sauce

75g (3oz) unsalted butter

1 garlic clove, crushed

450g (1lb) peeled and seeded pumpkin or butternut squash, cut into 1cm (½in) dice

1 tsp very finely chopped fresh rosemary leaves

finely grated zest of ½ lemon

freshly grated nutmeg

salt and freshly ground black pepper

Step one Put a large pan of well-salted water on to boil. When it is at a rolling boil, tip in the fusilli and cook until al dente (follow the packet instructions for timings). Drain.

Step two Meanwhile, melt the butter in a wide saucepan. Add the garlic and stir for about for 30 seconds or so, then add the diced pumpkin, rosemary, lemon zest, salt, pepper and nutmeg. Cover and sweat over a gentle heat for about 15 minutes, stirring occasionally, until the pumpkin is very soft. Squash a little of it down into the butter but leave about two-thirds more or less as it is. Taste and adjust the seasoning. Reheat if necessary once the pasta is cooked.

Step three Return the drained pasta to the pan, add the pumpkin sauce and mix lightly. Serve immediately, tucking a decorative sprig of rosemary, if using, into each helping. Pass around the grated Parmesan and enjoy!

Saffron and Pine Nut Pilaf

A lovely, golden pilaf perfumed with saffron and dotted with pine nuts. When serving this on its own, the garlicky yoghurt becomes a key player.

Step one To make the yoghurt relish, simply mix the yoghurt with the garlic, salt and pepper. Cover and chill until required.

Step two Preheat the oven to 150°C/300°F/gas 2. To make the pilaf, put the saffron in a small bowl, spoon over 2 tablespoons of the hot stock and leave to steep until needed. Fry the onion and garlic gently in 25g (1oz) of the butter in a heavy-based saucepan, without browning, until tender. Add the rice, bay leaf and cumin and coriander seeds and stir for about 1 minute. Pour in the remaining stock and season with salt and pepper. Bring to a gentle simmer, cover the pan tightly, reduce the heat as low as it will go and leave to cook, undisturbed, for 10 minutes.

Step three Meanwhile sauté the pine nuts in half the remaining butter until lightly browned. Check the rice – by now it should be just tender with a slight resistance to the bite, and all the liquid should have been absorbed. If not, uncover and let it boil off for a few minutes (but not too long – you don't want the rice to turn mushy). Stir in the parsley, dill and saffron.

Step four Turn the rice into a shallow dish, spoon over the pine nuts, dot with the last of the butter and cover the dish with silver foil. Pop the dish into the oven to steam the pilaf and keep it warm – it can stay there happily for half an hour or so.

Step five Just before dishing up, uncover and fluff up the grains of rice with a fork, turning them and breaking up any clumps. Serve straight away while still hot, accompanied by the cool yoghurt relish.

As a variation, try replacing the parsley and dill with 3 tablespoons chopped fresh coriander. Stir it in to the rice just before serving.

Serves 4

a generous pinch of saffron threads

600ml (1 pint) hot vegetable stock (see page 7)

1 large onion, chopped

1 garlic clove, chopped

75g (3oz) butter

250g (9oz) basmati rice, rinsed and thoroughly drained

1 bay leaf

2 tsp cumin seeds

2 tsp coriander seeds

75g (3oz) pine nuts

3 tbsp chopped fresh parsley

1 tbsp chopped fresh dill

for the yoghurt relish

200g (7oz) Greek yoghurt

3 garlic cloves, crushed

salt and freshly ground black pepper

Three-tomato Tart with Marjoram

This isn't quite a pizza, though it comes pretty close with its yeast dough and heavy complement of tomatoes. It is, in fact, constructed along the lines of a tart, with a bit more depth to it than a classic pizza. I first created this for the vegan boyfriend of a very dear old friend. As it happens, he had given up on veganism by the time he got to try it, but we all loved it.

Serves 4

2½ tbsp sun-dried tomato purée or red pesto

3 tbsp fine cornmeal or polenta

8 plum tomatoes, sliced

10 medium cherry tomatoes, halved

½ tsp fresh thyme leaves

½ tsp caster sugar

extra-virgin olive oil

a small handful of fresh marjoram, oregano or basil leaves

salt and pepper

for the yeast dough

225g (8oz) strong white bread flour

125g (4½oz) plain flour

1 tsp salt

1 x 7g sachet easy-blend dried yeast

1 generous tbsp extra-virgin olive oil

Step one To make the dough, sift the two flours into a bowl with the salt and stir in the yeast. Make a well in the centre and add the oil and enough water to make a soft dough. Knead vigorously for 5–10 minutes, until smooth and elastic. Place in an oiled bowl, turn to coat in oil, then cover with a damp tea towel and leave in a warm place for about 1 hour to rise until doubled in size. If you want to slow its progress down (the tart is nicest served warm from the oven, not reheated), then pop it into the fridge.

Step two Preheat the oven to 230°C/450°F/gas 8 and put a baking sheet inside. Oil a 25cm (10in) tart tin. Punch the dough down, knead it briefly, then spread it out thinly in the tin, pushing it up the sides. Spread the purée or pesto over the base. Sprinkle 1½ tablespoons of the cornmeal evenly over the purée. Now arrange the sliced plum tomatoes and halved cherry tomatoes, cut-sides up, haphazardly over the tart, covering the base completely and thickly. Sprinkle with the remaining cornmeal, the thyme leaves and sugar. Season well, then drizzle with 1½ tablespoons of olive oil, then let the tart sit for 10 minutes.

Step three Pop the tart onto the hot baking sheet and bake for 15 minutes, until the edges are puffed and golden brown. Brush the pastry with a little extra oil, then return to the oven for 5 minutes. Serve hot or warm, scattering over the fresh marjoram, oregano or basil just before taking the tart to the table.

For a slight change, try scattering a handful of Parmesan shavings (cut them from a block of Parmesan with a vegetable peeler) over the tart after it comes out of the oven.

Rice Salad with Apricots

I had oodles of rice left over from a huge vat that had been made to eat with our supper. It seemed a shame to waste it, so instead I dressed it up to make a lively rice salad to have for lunch. When I wrote out the recipe later on, I realized that the salad would have tasted even better if I had started on it as soon as the rice was cooked, so that the hot rice could absorb some of the dressing as it cooled. Either way, it tastes good, and is just the thing for a summer lunch or a barbecue.

Step one Cook the rice following the packet instructions. Meanwhile, make the dressing, by whisking the vinegar with the mustard, salt and pepper, then gradually whisking in the oil. Taste and adjust the seasoning, bearing in mind that it needs to be slightly sharper and saltier than usual to balance the blandness of the rice.

Step two Once the rice is cooked, tip it into a sieve and rinse with hot water, then leave to drain again. Tip the rice and dressing into a bowl and mix, then leave to cool – refrigerate if preparing the salad for the following day.

Step three To finish the salad, fry the onion and garlic gently in the oil until tender and translucent. Mix into the rice along with the spring onions, dried apricots and coriander. Taste again and adjust the seasoning if necessary.

Serves 4

about 350g (12oz) long-grain rice

1 small onion, finely chopped

1 garlic clove, finely chopped

1 tbsp sunflower or extra-virgin olive oil

6 spring onions, thinly sliced

75g (3oz) ready-to-eat dried apricots, finely diced

2–3 tbsp chopped fresh coriander

for the dressing

1½ tbsp white wine vinegar

½ tsp Dijon mustard

4 tbsp sunflower or extra-virgin olive oil

plenty of salt and freshly ground black pepper

Pearl Barley and Mushroom Risotto

The expression on my friend Fiona's face was hard to fathom as she tried a mouthful of this pearl barley risotto. Then suddenly she was all smiles. It turned out that as a child she had loathed the pearl barley that floated in bowls of Scotch broth. That had been her first taste of pearl barley in over 30 years, and she loved it! This has certainly become one of my hot-favourite new dishes for cool weather. It has all the flavour of a true risotto, but with the added advantage that it doesn't have to be stirred constantly. The disadvantage is that you must to remember to soak the pearl barley overnight, and then to precook it for 20 minutes. Although the dried porcini seem phenomenally expensive, a mere 15g (½oz) adds a big, big helping hand to the plainer button mushrooms.

Serves 6

350g (12oz) pearl barley, soaked overnight, then drained

15g (½ oz) dried porcini

600ml (1 pint) vegetable stock (see page 7)

1 onion, chopped

1 tbsp sunflower oil

40g (1½ oz) butter

2 garlic cloves, chopped

125g (4½ oz) button mushrooms, sliced

50ml (2fl oz) sweet sherry or Marsala

25g (1oz) Parmesan, freshly grated

2 tbsp finely chopped fresh flat-leaf parsley

salt and freshly ground black pepper

Step one Tip the barley into a pan of lightly salted boiling water and simmer for 20 minutes. Meanwhile, pour enough hot water over the dried porcini to cover. Leave to soak for 20 minutes.

Step two Remove the pieces of mushroom from the soaking liquid and chop roughly. Let the soaking liquid settle, then carefully pour it out of the bowl into a saucepan, leaving any grit behind. Add the stock and bring to the boil.

Step three Cook the onion gently in the sunflower oil and 15g (½oz) of the butter in a large deep frying pan or wide, shallow saucepan. When it is tender, add the garlic, porcini and sliced button mushrooms. Fry for about 4 minutes, or until the mushrooms have softened. Now tip in the barley, stir briefly, then pour in the sherry or Marsala. Stir for about 2 minutes, until the liquid has virtually evaporated. Now add the boiling stock, all in one fell swoop, season and leave to simmer gently for about 15–20 minutes until most of the liquid has been absorbed and the barley is tender.

Step four Stir in the remaining butter, plus the Parmesan and parsley, then taste and adjust seasoning. Serve immediately.

Tagliatelle with Rocket Pesto and Grilled Red Pepper

When my son was four years old he discovered real pesto in San Gimignano. When we came home he longed for more, so I spooned some store-bought pesto onto his pasta. He was not amused. Chastened, I took once again to making it. He took strongly to this rocket pesto, too. It is made the same way as traditional pesto and, like the standard basil pesto, it makes a powerful, vivid green cream. It is brilliant with pasta but try spreading a little on toasted bread. Top it with goats' cheese and grill until the cheese is browned; or toss it with boiled new potatoes.

Step one To make the pesto, put all the ingredients except the olive oil into the bowl of a food processor and process to a paste. With the motor still running, gradually trickle in the oil until you have a thick cream. Scrape into a small bowl.

Step two Cook the pasta in boiling, salted water according to packet instructions. When it is nearly done, sauté the grilled peppers in the olive oil for a few minutes to heat through. Drain the pasta thoroughly, then toss with about half the pesto. Taste and add a little more if you wish. Top with the strips of pepper and serve immediately, with freshly grated Parmesan.

If you're not planning to use the pesto immediately, put it into a screwtop jar, cover with a thin layer of olive oil, then seal tightly and store in the fridge. As long as it's covered with oil and refrigerated, it will keep for a week or more.

Serves 4

400–450g (14oz–1lb) tagliatelle or spaghetti

3 red peppers (or use red and yellow peppers), grilled, skinned (see page 67), seeded and cut into strips

2 tbsp extra-virgin olive oil

freshly grated Parmesan, to serve

for the pesto

110g (4oz) rocket leaves, roughly torn

50g (2oz) lightly toasted hazelnuts

2–3 garlic cloves, roughly chopped

50g (2oz) pecorino or Parmesan, roughly broken into chunks

125ml (4fl oz) extra-virgin olive oil

salt and freshly ground black pepper

Penne o Fusilli alla Vesuviana

Vesuvius dominates Naples and the Amalfi coast, towering over them, dormant but not dead. It has created two of the greatest, most heart-rending sites in the world, Pompeii and Herculaneum. More cheerily, from its fertile but perilous slopes comes a rather special pasta dish, combining juicy, scarlet tomatoes with the milky, tender buffalo mozzarella made nearby, and sharp, full-tasting matured pecorino.

Serves 4

400–450g (14oz–1lb) dried fusilli, penne or other pasta shapes

5 tbsp extra-virgin olive oil

500g (1lb 2oz) ripest, most fully flavoured tomatoes, skinned, seeded and chopped

1 tbsp tomato purée

½ tsp caster sugar

125g (4½ oz) buffalo-milk mozzarella, drained and diced

50g (2oz) pecorino or Parmesan, freshly grated

1 level tsp dried oregano

small handful fresh basil leaves, roughly torn

salt and freshly ground black pepper

Step one Bring a large pan of well-salted water to a rolling boil and tip in the pasta. Bring back to the boil and cook until al dente (follow the packet instructions for timings).

Step two As soon as you have got the pasta into the water, heat up the olive oil. Add the tomatoes, tomato purée, sugar, and a little salt and pepper. Cook briskly for about 2 minutes, then add the mozzarella, grated pecorino or Parmesan and oregano. Stir, then cover and cook over a low heat until the pasta is done (about 6–7 minutes). Drain the pasta and return to the pan.

Step three Spoon the sauce over the pasta, mix thoroughly over a gentle heat, then add the basil and serve immediately.

If you want to echo the dangers of the volcano, try adding one or two hot red chillies to the sauce.

Pasta and Rice Pilaf

This Greek-style pilaf can be served as a side dish, a super-rice for backing up main dishes, with or without plenty of sauce (in which case cooking it with water is fine). If you have some really excellent home-made vegetable stock, with oodles of flavour, however, using it will transform the pilaf into a dish that is fine enough to enjoy as a star turn in its own right.

Step one Rinse the rice well and then leave it to drain thoroughly. Heat the olive oil with a third of the butter in a heavy-based pan large enough to take all the ingredients. Add the spring onions (make sure you include their green parts as well as the white) and sauté for 1–2 minutes, until they wilt. Add the orzo and fry for about 2 minutes. Tip in the rice and fry for a further minute or so. Next, add the stock, cinnamon stick and bay leaf and season with salt and pepper. Bring to the boil and then reduce the heat as low as it will go. Cover tightly and leave, undisturbed, for 10 minutes. By then the rice and pasta should be tender and should have absorbed all the liquid (if not, uncover and raise the heat so that what's left can boil off).

Step two If you want to eat immediately, stir in the remaining butter and serve. If you have time, tip the pilaf into a shallow dish, dot with the remaining butter, cover with foil and then place in a preheated low oven (around 150°C/300°F/gas 2) and leave for 20 minutes, to steam gently and steadily in its own moisture. Uncover, fluff up with a fork and serve.

Occasionally, supermarkets stock the small 'grains' of pasta (which may be labelled orzo, the Italian for barley), but you are more likely to locate it in a Greek or Italian delicatessen. Failing that, snip pasta into short lengths with scissors. Hold the ends of the pasta inside a clear plastic bag and poke the scissors inside to cut them, otherwise they fly about everywhere.

Serves 4–6

150g (5oz) long-grain rice (basmati is perfect)

1 tbsp extra virgin olive oil

40g (1¼ oz) butter

8 spring onions, chopped

150g (5oz) orzo (rice-shaped pasta)

850ml (1½ pints) vegetable stock (see page 7)

1 cinnamon stick

1 bay leaf

salt and freshly ground black pepper

Chestnut and Celery Risotto

This risotto, with its felicitous marriage of mealy sweet chestnut and firm, savoury celery, is a way of using fresh chestnuts that I recommend with considerable enthusiasm. I know that peeling chestnuts is one of the worst of all kitchen tasks but there is, honestly, nothing to match the taste of the fresh nuts, and once or maybe twice a year it's worth doing. If you really can't face it, or just don't have time, vacuum-packed chestnuts in tins or plastic packs are an acceptable, second-rung alternative. As with any risotto, the rice must be proper risotto rice, such as arborio, vialone nano or carnaroli. The stock must be real, too, as ready-made stock cubes do this dish no favours at all.

Serves 5–6

275g (10oz) fresh chestnuts

850 ml–1.2 litres (1½–2 pints) good-quality vegetable stock (see page 7)

50g (2oz) butter

1 small onion, chopped

2 garlic cloves, chopped

225g (8oz) arborio or other Italian risotto rice

8 celery sticks, sliced into thin crescents

2 fresh thyme sprigs

1 fresh sage leaf

3 tbsp freshly grated Parmesan

salt and freshly ground black pepper

1 tbsp chopped fresh flat-leaf parsley, to garnish

Step one Score an 'X' on the rounded side of each chestnut, cutting right through the tough outer skin. Put 4 or 5 chestnuts at a time into a microwavable bowl, cover tightly with clingfilm and microwave on full for 1–2 minutes until the skins have split open. While they are still hot, peel the chestnuts, removing the inner as well as the outer skin. Repeat with the remaining chestnuts until all are done. Don't be tempted to cook more of them at once as they become harder to peel as they cool down. Break the peeled chestnuts into large pieces.

Step two Bring the stock to the boil in a pan and keep hot. Meanwhile, melt half the butter in a large, heavy pan. Add the onion and garlic and cook until tender, without browning. Add the rice and celery to the onion and stir until the rice turns translucent. Now stir in the chestnuts, thyme, sage, salt and pepper and 150ml (5fl oz) of the hot stock. Simmer over a low heat, stirring continuously, until the stock has been absorbed. Add another 150ml (5fl oz) of stock and continue stirring until absorbed. Repeat until the rice is tender but still has a bite to it. The risotto should be creamy but not swimming in liquid.

Step three Stir in the remaining butter and the Parmesan. Taste and adjust the seasoning. Sprinkle with the chopped fresh parsley and serve.

Green Summer Risotto

This is a summer risotto par excellence, but choose a day that is not too hot to make it, so that stirring the risotto becomes pleasantly meditative rather than a sweaty endurance test.

Step one Heat 15g (½oz) of the butter and the olive oil in a frying pan and sauté the diced courgettes over a high heat, until tender and patched with brown. Reserve.

Step two If they are fresh, blanch the broad beans in boiling water for 1–2 minutes and then drain. No need to blanch thawed frozen beans. Using a small, sharp knife, slit each bean open and squeeze out the vivid green beanlet inside. Discard the skins. Now finish the cooking in fresh, lightly salted water, and drain.

Step three Put the stock into a pan and bring gently to the boil, then turn the heat down as low as it will go, to keep the stock hot without letting it boil quite away.

Step four Heat 25g (1oz) of the butter in a wide pan over a low–moderate heat. Add the onion and grated courgette. Fry until both are tender but not browning. Add the rice and stir it about with the courgette and onion for 1 minute, until it turns translucent. Pour in the white wine, add the parsley, season and stir until the wine has almost all evaporated. Next, add a ladleful of the hot stock and keep stirring until that has been absorbed. Keep adding the stock in the same way until the rice is al dente (tender but with a slight resistance to the bite). Should you run out of stock, start adding boiling-hot water. At this point, the risotto should still be fairly wet but not swimming in a lake of liquid.

Step five Stir in the broad beans and the diced courgettes and cook for a further 1–2 minutes, to heat them through. Now draw the pan off the heat and stir in the chopped herbs, the remainder of the butter and the Parmesan. Taste and adjust the seasoning and serve straight away.

Serves 3–4

50g (2oz) butter

1 tbsp extra-virgin olive oil

450g (1lb) courgettes, one-third coarsely grated, two-thirds diced

250g (9oz) shelled broad beans (ideally fresh, or frozen and thawed)

850ml–1.2 litres (1½–2 pints) vegetable stock (see page 7)

1 onion, chopped

225g (8oz) arborio or other Italian risotto rice

1 glass white wine

2 tbsp chopped fresh flat-leaf parsley

small handful of fresh basil leaves, torn

2 tbsp snipped fresh chives

½ tbsp chopped fresh tarragon (optional)

2 tbsp chopped fresh mint

25g (1oz) Parmesan, freshly grated

salt and freshly ground black pepper

Pasta alla Genovese

On my first visit to Genoa I wanted above all to taste real pesto in its native territory. We found a small restaurant with a terrace, sipped ice-cold Campari soda, and then revelled in big bowlfuls of *trofie* – small, thick, hand-made pasta gnocchi – bathed in the brilliant green nectar. Some years later, I was introduced to another, equally authentic version of pasta with pesto. This time it was ordinary spaghetti (dried, not fresh), cooked with pieces of carrot, potato and green bean in the same pan, then drenched in pesto.

Serves 4

400–450g (14oz–1lb) dried spaghetti (not quick-cooking)

1–2 large potatoes, peeled and roughly cut into 2cm (¾in) chunks

2–3 carrots, thickly sliced

125g (4½oz) green beans, cut into 4cm (1½in) lengths

plenty of salt

freshly grated pecorino or Parmesan, to serve

for the pesto

75g (3oz) fresh basil leaves

50g (2oz) hard pecorino or Parmesan, or a mixture of the two, broken into chunks

50g (2oz) pine nuts

2–3 garlic cloves, roughly chopped

110–125ml (4–4½fl oz) extra-virgin olive oil

Step one To make the pesto, put the basil leaves, cheese, pine nuts and garlic into a food processor and process to a paste. With the motor still running, trickle in the olive oil to give a creamy sauce. (If you want to do it in a less machine-driven way, put the garlic and a pinch or two of salt into a mortar or heavy bowl and pound it to a paste using a pestle or the end of a rolling pin. Add the basil and nuts and keep pounding until you have a green paste. Grate the cheese and add that too, working it in with the pestle. Then work in enough olive oil to give a creamy sauce.)

Step two Bring a large pan of well-salted water to the boil and add the spaghetti, potatoes and carrots. About half way through the cooking time (check the packet instructions), add the beans. By the time the pasta is al dente the vegetables will be cooked.

Step three Drain the pasta well, return to the pan and toss with the pesto. Serve with grated pecorino or Parmesan.

Potato Gnocchi with Fennel and Sun-dried Tomato Butter

Gnocchi make a grand first or main course, dressed as they are here.

Step one Weigh out exactly 1kg (2¼lb) of the potato purée and put it in a bowl. Make a well in the centre and add the egg, flour, nutmeg, salt and pepper. Work together thoroughly to make a soft, warm dough. Cover with a tea towel. Flour 3 baking trays generously. Break off tennis-ball-sized knobs of the dough and roll out to form long sausages about the thickness of your thumb. Cut into pieces 2.5cm (1in) long.

Step two Take a fork and hold it with the tip of the tines down on the work surface, their outer curve facing upwards. With the tip of a finger, lightly press a piece of the dough against the tines, right at the bottom. In one swift movement roll and flip the dough up and off the fork, so that one side is ridged from the tines, while the other has an indentation from the tip of your finger. You don't need to take the piece of dough far up the tines – just enough to imprint the ridges on one side only. As you make them, spread the gnocchi out on the floured trays. Once made, cover with a clean tea towel until needed.

Step three Put a large pan of salted water on to boil. Melt the butter in a medium frying pan and add the garlic. Fry gently until it just begins to colour. Add the sun-dried tomatoes, olives and fennel. Stir for about 2 minutes, then draw off the heat.

Step four When the water reaches a rolling boil, drop one-quarter to one-third of the gnocchi into it. When they bob back to the surface, check one to make sure it is cooked. Quickly lift out the rest with a perforated spoon. Place in a warm dish and keep warm while you cook the remaining gnocchi.

Step five Reheat the sauce and then spoon it over the gnocchi. Scatter with shavings of pecorino or Parmesan and serve.

Serves 4–6

for the gnocchi

1.5kg (3lb) floury potatoes, peeled, boiled and rubbed, still warm, through a potato ricer, mouli legumes or sieve

1 egg

250g (9oz) plain flour, sifted, plus extra for dusting

freshly grated nutmeg

salt and pepper

fine shavings of pecorino or Parmesan, to serve

for the butter sauce

150g (5oz) unsalted butter

4 garlic cloves, thinly sliced

50g (2oz) sun-dried tomatoes in olive oil, very finely shredded

50g (2oz) black olives, pitted and sliced

3 tbsp chopped fennel leaf

Glazed Carrots with Cinnamon and Lemon Thyme

Lemon thyme and cinnamon together bring out the best in carrots. A sprig of thyme cooked with the carrots imparts a hint of its flavour right to their core, while a final dressing of lemon thyme leaves brings a second fresh dose.

Serves 4

600g (1lb 4oz) carrots, thickly sliced

40g (1½ oz) butter

40g (1½ oz) granulated or caster sugar

1 cinnamon stick

1 fresh lemon thyme sprig

¾–1 tsp fresh lemon thyme leaves

salt

Step one Put all the ingredients except the lemon thyme leaves into a pan with almost, but not quite, enough water to cover the carrots. Bring to the boil, then leave to simmer, uncovered, for about 12 minutes, stirring occasionally, by which time the carrots should be tender (and I mean tender, not al dente). Scoop them out and reserve.

Step two Boil the liquid hard until it is reduced to a thin layer of syrup on the bottom of the pan (if you are short of time, transfer the liquid to a wide frying pan to speed the process up, but take care that it doesn't burn). Return the carrots to the pan and turn them in the syrup, coating them well, until piping hot.

Step three Remove the thyme sprig and cinnamon stick, then stir in the reserved lemon thyme leaves. Taste and adjust the seasoning, then serve.

Rosemary Roast Potatoes

These are just the best-ever roast potatoes. Anointed with olive oil and cut small so there's twice as much crispness, they are lightly flavoured with garlic and rosemary.

Step one Preheat the oven to 200°C/400°F/gas 6. Peel the potatoes and cut into chunks about 3cm (generous 1in) across. Cook in boiling, salted water for about 4–5 minutes, or until not quite cooked. Drain thoroughly and scratch criss-cross lines all over the surfaces of each chunk with the tines of a fork, to rough up the outside – this makes for a much crisper exterior.

Step two Put the potatoes, garlic, rosemary and salt into a roasting tin large enough to take them in a compact single layer, and pour over the olive oil. Turn them all together with your fingers, so that each piece of potato is coated in oil. Roast for 45–55 minutes, turning the potatoes after the first 30 minutes (no earlier, or they may stick to the tin), and then again once or twice more, until they are crisp and patched with brown. Serve immediately.

Serves 4–6

about 1.5kg (3lb) large waxy potatoes, e.g. Cara, or end-of-season new potatoes

10 whole garlic cloves, unpeeled

4 large fresh rosemary sprigs

6 tbsp extra-virgin olive oil

salt

Winter Squash and Feta Gratin

There's something almost magical about the pairing of sweet orange winter squash with salty Mediterranean cheeses like feta and Italian parmesan. Baked until the edges brown in the heat, this gratin works equally well as a side dish or a light main course, hot or warm.

Serves 4–8

2kg (4½ lb) winter squash (pumpkin will do, but butternut, red kuri, crown prince or onion squash are much better)

50g (2oz) butter

150g (5oz) feta, drained and chopped or crumbled

75g (3oz) freshly grated Parmesan

110g (4oz) breadcrumbs

3 tbsp extra-virgin olive oil

salt and freshly ground black pepper

Step one Preheat the oven to 200°C/400°F/gas 6. Halve the squash if it is a whole one, then remove the fibrous mass of seeds. Cut into long slices about 2.5–4cm (1–1½in) thick. You can cut the skin from the slices now, or after the initial cooking, which I think is marginally easier and quicker. Bring a large pan of salted water to the boil, then add the squash slices (you may have to cook them in two batches). Bring back to the boil and then simmer for about 5–10 minutes, until the flesh is just tender (but not soggy). Drain thoroughly, then remove the skin, if you haven't already.

Step two Use a generous knob of the butter to grease a shallow ovenproof dish (I use a 35cm/14in gratin dish). Arrange the squash in it, scattering the crumbled feta over the squash as you go. Dot with the remaining butter, then season with salt and plenty of pepper. Mix the Parmesan with the breadcrumbs and scatter evenly over the squash. Drizzle the olive oil over the top. Bake for about 30 minutes, turning the dish around half-way through cooking if necessary, until evenly browned and crisp on top. Serve hot or warm.

Fagioli all'Uccelletto (Beans in Tomato and Sage Sauce)

Fagioli all'uccelletto is possibly the nicest of all Tuscan bean dishes, and there are plenty to choose from. Sort of like superior baked beans, Italian style, they are actually simmered, rather than baked, in a tomato sauce flavoured with browned garlic and sage. The name itself means 'beans cooked in the style of little birds', though quite what it has to do with little birds, no one seems terribly sure. Anyway, the final dish is terrific – certainly good enough to eat on its own with slices of toasted country bread, and maybe a green salad, for a light lunch or supper.

Step one Drain the soaked beans, then place in a pan with enough water to cover generously. Don't add any salt. Bring to the boil, boil hard for 10 minutes, then reduce the heat and simmer gently until tender (anything from 40 minutes to 1½ hours, depending on the age of the beans) adding more hot water if needed. Drain.

Step two Fry the garlic and sage leaves gently in the oil. When the garlic is golden brown, add the beans and season generously. Add the sieved tomatoes or passata, and the tomato purée, and about 1 teaspoon of caster sugar, if necessary. Simmer gently for a further 20 minutes or so, stirring occasionally to prevent catching. Check and adjust the seasoning just before serving.

If you don't have the time or will to cook the beans from dry, then you can substitute 500g (1lb 2oz) tinned cannellini or haricot beans.

Serves 4–5

250g (9oz) dried white haricot or cannellini beans, soaked overnight

3 garlic cloves, finely chopped

6 fresh sage leaves

3 tbsp extra-virgin olive oil, plus a little extra for serving

350g (12oz) very ripe, soft tomatoes, puréed in a liquidizer or food processor then sieved, or 310g (11oz) passata

1 tbsp tomato purée

sugar, if needed

salt and freshly ground black pepper

155

Preserved Lemons

For me, the most exciting taste in all of Moroccan cooking is that of salt-preserved lemons. There is nothing else quite like it.

Fills a 1 litre (1¾ pint) preserving jar

50–75g (2–3oz) coarse salt

8 unwaxed lemons

2 bay leaves (optional)

Step one Sterilize a 1 litre (1¾ pint) preserving jar. Preheat the oven to 110°C/225°F/gas ¼. Wash the jar in soapy water, then rinse in warm water. Without touching the inside of the jar, place it upside down on a rack in the oven and leave for 30 minutes. Remove from the oven and cool, covered with a clean tea towel. Sprinkle a heaped tablespoonful of the salt over the base.

Step two Take a lemon and make 2 cuts at right angles, starting from the stem end and finishing about 1cm (½in) short of the other end, so the lemon is cut almost into quarters, but still holds together. Open the fruit out a little and sprinkle the insides generously with salt, then reshape the lemon. Pack it down firmly in the preserving jar. Sprinkle with salt. Repeat with another four lemons, pressing each one down firmly, so that they all squash into the jar and release some of their juice.

Step three Pour in the juice of the remaining 3 lemons, and add enough water to cover all the lemons in the jar completely. If you like, tuck a couple of bay leaves down the sides of the jar.

Step four Now cut 2 lengths of wooden skewer just a touch longer than the diameter of the opening of the jar. Push them down under the rim of the jar, at right angles to each other, so that they force the lemons to remain submerged. Seal the jar tightly and leave for about 4 weeks before using.

Step five When you need a lemon for a recipe, remove it from the lemon brine with a wooden spoon (not a metal one, which could discolour and taint the remaining lemons). Separate the quarters, cut away the inner pulp and discard. Cut the peel into strips. The tart brine is useful too – excellent in salad dressings or in marinades.

Naan Bread with Coriander Pesto

I'd better warn you straight away that these do not turn out like the naan bread that you get in Indian restaurants, but they taste even better.

Step one Put the flour into a bowl with the salt and yeast and mix evenly. Add the oil and rub it in as though you were making pastry. Add enough water to mix to a soft, very slightly sticky dough. Turn it out and knead vigorously, dusting with a little extra flour if necessary, for a good 5–10 minutes, until smooth and elastic. Return to the bowl, cover with a damp cloth and leave in a warm place for about 1 hour until doubled in size.

Step two Meanwhile, make the coriander pesto. Put the coriander leaves, toasted hazelnuts, garlic and creamed coconut into a food processor with some salt and pepper. Process until smooth, then, with the motor still running, gradually trickle in the oil to form a smooth, thick sauce. Taste and adjust the seasoning, exaggerating it a touch.

Step three When the dough has risen, punch it back, knead briefly, then divide into 6. Roll each piece into a ball on a floured surface, then roll out as thinly as you can to form a circle about 15cm (6in) across. Smear a tablespoon of pesto over one half, leaving a 1cm (½in) border around the edge. Brush the border with water, then fold the dough in half to cover the pesto entirely. Pinch the edges together firmly, then roll the naan out again to form a pointed oval, about 20cm (8in) long. Don't worry too much if a bit of the pesto squidges out, but aim to keep most of it inside.

Step four Place a heavy-based frying pan or griddle over a medium-high heat. Let it heat up for about 4 minutes, then lay the first naan on it and cook for 30–60 seconds, until it is beginning to puff and the underneath is spotted with brown dots. Turn over and cook the other side in the same way. Keep warm, loosely covered, in a warm oven, while you cook the other naan breads.

Makes 6

450g (1lb) strong white bread flour, plus extra for dusting

1 tsp salt

1 x 7g sachet easy-blend dried yeast

2 tbsp sunflower oil

for the pesto

½ big bunch of fresh coriander, stalks discarded, leaves only (you need about 50–60g/2 2⅛ oz)

50g (2oz) hazelnuts, lightly toasted

3 garlic cloves, roughly chopped

40g (1½ oz) creamed coconut, roughly chopped

75ml (3fl oz) sunflower or vegetable oil

salt and freshly ground black pepper

Spinach with Seville Orange and Breadcrumbs

The spicy sourness of Seville oranges adds a wonderful zest to spinach, but sadly their season is short. There is, however, a year-round alternative, though it is not quite the same. When the marmalade-making season is over, substitute the juice of half a lemon mixed with the juice of half an ordinary orange for the Seville orange juice, and serve with wedges of orange.

Serves 4

1kg (2¼ lb) fresh spinach

40g (1½ oz) butter

1 tbsp sunflower oil

15g (½ oz) fine dry breadcrumbs

juice of 1 Seville orange

1 tsp ground cinnamon

salt and freshly ground black pepper

4 wedges of Seville orange, to serve

Step one Wash the spinach thoroughly and discard any thick tough stems or damaged leaves. Shake off excess water, and pack the spinach into a large pan. Cover and cook over a gentle heat for 5 minutes. Stir, cover again, then turn the heat up slightly and cook for a further 5–10 minutes, stirring occasionally until the spinach is just cooked. Drain well.

Step two Heat 15g (½oz) of butter and the oil in a small frying pan and fry the breadcrumbs until golden brown. Drain on kitchen paper. Just before serving, reheat the spinach with the remaining butter, orange juice, cinnamon, salt and pepper, stirring as it heats up. Taste and adjust the seasonings. At the same time, reheat the breadcrumbs.

Step three Tip the spinach into a warm serving dish and scatter the crumbs over the top. Serve with the orange wedges.

Rice and Peas

Rice and Peas is one of the great Caribbean staples. The peas are actually beans, traditionally pigeon peas, but black-eyed beans make an honourable substitute (and need no pre-soaking). Kidney beans are good too.

Step one Pigeon peas and black-eyed beans need no soaking. Kidney beans will need to be soaked overnight. Put the beans, drained if they have been soaked, into a large pan with plenty of water (no salt at this stage), then bring to the boil. Boil hard for 15 minutes, then reduce the heat and simmer until the beans are tender. Drain and set aside.

Step two Cook the rice in boiling, salted water until almost tender but still slightly chalky in the centre, then drain. Mix the rice with the peas or beans, spring onions and creamed coconut. Now rinse the pan out and pour in enough water just to cover the base and no more. Tip in the rice mixture and dot with the butter. Lay a clean tea towel over the top, then cover with the lid, so that you have a very snug fit, lifting the trailing ends of cloth up over the lid so that they don't go up in flames. Cook over a low heat for 5 minutes or so, to steam the rice until perfectly tender. Fluff the rice up with a fork, then taste and adjust the seasoning.

Serves 4

110g (4oz) dried pigeon peas, black-eyed beans or red kidney beans

310g (11oz) long-grain rice

3 spring onions, chopped

50g (2oz) creamed coconut, grated or chopped

15g (½ oz) butter

salt

For more recipes from My Kitchen Table, sign up for our newsletter at www.mykitchentable.co.uk/newsletter

163

Loud Mash

Make the mash in advance by all means, but don't stir in the beetroot until the last minute or it will discolour. The beetroot can be boiled but I prefer to bake them, wrapped individually in silver foil, in a low to moderate oven (the exact temperature doesn't matter that much but see page 56 for detailed instructions) for several hours, until the skin scrapes away easily from the stalk end.

Serves 4

around 350g (12oz) cooked beetroot, peeled (see page 56)

600g (1lb 4oz) floury potatoes, boiled until tender, then peeled

25g (1oz) butter

150–300ml (¼–½ pint) whole milk

freshly grated nutmeg

salt and freshly ground black pepper

Step one Grate the cooked beetroot (use a food processor if possible – it makes for a far less messy undertaking). Mash the potatoes in the pan while still warm, with the butter and seasoning. Place over a moderate heat and gradually whisk in enough milk to form a soft, creamy mash.

Step two If necessary, reheat the potatoes just before serving. Stir in the beetroot, taste and adjust the seasoning.

Mint, Grape and Cucumber Raita

Greek tzatziki meets Indian raita with a sunny hint of Mediterranean sweetness from the grapes. Serve this yoghurty side dish as a soothing, harmonizing addition to a spicy main course.

Step one Put the cucumber into a colander and sprinkle lightly with salt. Leave to drain for 30 minutes, then rinse and pat dry on kitchen paper.

Step two Stir the cucumber into the yoghurt with the grapes. Shred 14 of the mint leaves and stir those in too, then season with pepper. Taste and adjust the seasoning, adding salt only if you feel it really needs it.

Step three Just before serving, stir the raita again and spoon into a serving dish. Garnish with a light dusting of paprika and the reserved mint leaves.

½ cucumber, peeled and finely diced

250g (9oz) Greek-style yoghurt

25 seedless white grapes, quartered

16 fresh mint leaves

a pinch of paprika, to garnish

salt and freshly ground black pepper

167

French Beans with Cumin and Almonds

Who would have thought that adding a spoonful of cumin and a few almonds to a panful of French beans would turn them into something so exotic? Well, it does, though they're not so over-the-top exotic as to clash with an otherwise straightforward meal.

Serves 4

2 tbsp olive or sunflower oil or 25g (1oz) butter

15g (½oz) flaked almonds

1 small onion, chopped

450g (1lb) French beans, topped, tailed and cut into 2.5–4cm (1–1½in) lengths

1 tsp ground cumin

salt and freshly ground black pepper

Step one Heat the oil or butter in a wide frying pan. Fry the almonds briskly until golden brown. Scoop out and drain on kitchen paper.

Step two Reduce the heat under the pan and fry the onions until tender, without browning. Add the beans, cumin and salt and pepper and fry for 3 minutes. Add 2 tablespoons of water, then cover and cook for 5 minutes or so until the beans are tender and most of the liquid has been absorbed.

Step three Return the almonds to the pan, stir for a few seconds to reheat, and serve.

Wild Garlic Mash

This is really a springtime play on the Irish theme of mash with greens, but instead of the spring onions or cabbage, I've used the gloriously pongy wild garlic that comes absolutely free in the springtime. If you have ever wandered through a wood at bluebell time and remarked on the pervasive reek of garlic, and perhaps noticed beautiful white flowers on slender stems, surrounded by leaves that could almost be those of a hyacinth, or tulip, then you have been amongst wild garlic. It grows in woods and damp hedgerows (there's a lovely vigorous patch just on the edge of the village road, five minutes' walk from our house). The tender leaves poke their heads up in March, and come into flower in late April or May. Only pick it if you are sure you know what it is, and always double check that it does indeed carry a powerful scent of garlic. When young and tender, the leaves are great shredded in salads. By the time the flowers appear, they are better lightly cooked.

Step one Either bake the potatoes or cook them in the microwave. If you must boil them, leave them whole and cook in their skins so that they don't absorb too much water. While they cook, rinse the garlic leaves, dry them as well as you can, then shred finely.

Step two When the potatoes are done, and while they are still hot, if possible, scoop out the flesh (or skin them, if boiled) into a saucepan. Add half the butter, season with salt, and then mash or beat the potatoes over a moderate heat (a hand-held electric whisk does the job most efficiently, but don't go on for too long or you'll end up with a gluey texture), gradually adding enough hot milk to give the kind of consistency you prefer; I like mashed potatoes verging on runny, but not everyone does.

Step three Melt the remaining butter in a frying pan over a moderate heat and sauté the wild garlic in it very briefly until wilted. Stir into the steaming-hot mash. Taste and adjust the seasoning.

Serves 4

1kg (2¼ lb) floury main-crop potatoes

2 large handfuls (about 150g/5oz) wild garlic leaves

40g (1½ oz) butter

150ml–300ml (¼–½ pint) hot milk

salt

171

Sophie's Spinaci alla Genovese (Spinach with Garlic, Pine Nuts and Raisins)

Traditonally, this Italian and Spanish way of cooking spinach with pine nuts and raisins includes anchovies, but it tastes good without. Jettisoning tradition altogether, I cook it at high speed in a wok.

Serves 4

700g (1½lb) fresh spinach

4 tbsp extra-virgin olive oil

2 garlic cloves, finely chopped

50g (2oz) raisins or currants

50g (2oz) pine nuts

freshly grated nutmeg

salt and freshly ground black pepper

Step one Rinse the spinach thoroughly, then pat dry on kitchen paper or a clean tea towel. This quantity of spinach will need to be cooked in two batches, so divide the spinach and all the other ingredients in half, and arrange next to the hob.

Step two Put a large wok over a high heat and leave until it smokes. Add half the olive oil, and then add half the garlic. Stir-fry for a few seconds, then add half the spinach, half the raisins or currants, half the pine nuts, and salt, pepper and nutmeg. Stir-fry briskly for a few minutes, until the spinach has begun to wilt and soften. Scoop out immediately into a warm serving dish. Quickly repeat the whole process with the rest of the ingredients. Taste and adjust the seasoning and serve immediately.

Parchment-baked New Potatoes with Chinese Chives

This neat, pretty way of cooking new potatoes in a wrapper of greaseproof paper is something of a classic, and it produces gloriously buttery, tender little mouthfuls. The flavour of Chinese chives (particularly the flower-bud stems) is very good with them, though thyme, rosemary and parsley can all be used instead.

Step one Preheat the oven to 190°C/375°F/gas 5. Cut out 2 large, heart-shaped pieces of greaseproof paper (they should be around 32cm (13in) across at the widest part and around 28cm (11in) in length). Lay each one half on a baking tray.

Step two Put half the potatoes on each piece of paper. Dot with the butter, sprinkle with the chives or other herbs and season with coarse salt. Fold the other half of the heart over to form a skewed semi-circle. Starting at the pointed end, seal the edges pressing them over and over again. Work your way around each package to enclose the potatoes neatly and snugly.

Step three Bake for 35 minutes, by which time the potatoes will be tender and buttery. Serve immediately in their parcels, so that they can be opened at the table.

Serves 3–4

500g (1lb 2oz) small new potatoes (about 16–20 potatoes)

40–50g (1½–2oz) butter

2 tbsp roughly chopped Chinese chives or thyme, rosemary or parsley leaves

coarse salt

Guacamole

Guacamole, essentially mashed avocados gleefully spiced up, is an incredibly useful sort of a food. It is a great starter with nothing more than strips of warm pitta bread and raw vegetables to dip into it, but it slides easily into the role of sauce or relish and is also very good spooned on to baked potatoes.

Serves 4

¼ red onion, chopped

2 garlic cloves, chopped

3 tbsp roughly chopped fresh coriander, plus a few leaves to garnish

1–2 green or red chillies, seeded and finely chopped

2–3 ripe avocados, depending on size

2 tomatoes, skinned, seeded and finely chopped

juice of ½–1 lime

a pinch of sugar

salt and freshly ground black pepper

a sprinkling of cayenne pepper, to serve

Step one Mix the onion, garlic, coriander and chillies on a chopping board and chop together very finely (or whizz them together in brief spurts in a food processor, watching that you don't end up with a purée).

Step two Peel and stone the avocados and mash with a potato masher or fork (but don't put them in the food processor, as you want to end up with a slightly uneven mush, though it shouldn't be positively lumpy). Mix the avocados with the chopped flavourings, tomatoes, juice of half the lime, a pinch of sugar and salt and black pepper. Taste and add more lime juice if needed. There should be just enough to take the edge off the richness of the avocado without making it too tart.

Step three Scoop into a bowl, smooth down and cover the surface of the guacamole with clingfilm to keep the air out as much as possible and so delay browning. Just before serving, give it a light stir to reveal the vivid colour of the purée, then scatter with a little extra coriander and a very light dusting of cayenne pepper.

Compote of Apples and Raisins with Nutmeg and Greek-style Yoghurt

This compote of apples and raisins is one that we make in copious quantities every year when the apples ripen in our garden. We eat it for pudding and for breakfast, and it can be used as a pie or tart filling as well, if the fancy takes you. It can be made several days in advance, and served warm or cold. The mild creamy tartness of Greek-style yoghurt balances the sweetness.

Serves 4

100g (4oz) caster sugar

75g (3oz) light muscovado sugar

about 500g (1lb 2oz) good eating apples, peeled, cored and cut into eigths

50g (2oz) raisins

freshly grated nutmeg

4 tbsp Greek-style yoghurt, to serve

Step one Put all the sugar into a pan with 425ml (¾ pint) water and stir over a moderate heat until completely dissolved. Bring to the boil, then add the apples and raisins and a grating of nutmeg. Simmer very gently for about 30 minutes, until the apple slices are translucent and very tender.

Step two Scoop the apples out into a shallow dish or bowl using a slotted spoon and add another fresh grating of nutmeg. Boil the juice down for 3–4 minutes, until syrupy, then pour it over the apples. Serve warm or cold, with the yoghurt.

Bay-scented Baked Custard with Apricot Jam and Clotted Cream

In this divinely rich pudding the custard is infused with bay and topped with thin layers of apricot jam and clotted cream – bliss! Make the custards the day before they are to be eaten, or at least in the morning for the evening, so that they have time to cool and chill before anyone slips their eager spoon down through the layers.

Serves 6

300ml (½ pint) single, whipping or double cream

150ml (¼ pint) milk

2 bay leaves

4 egg yolks

40g (1½oz) vanilla sugar (or caster sugar and ½ tsp vanilla extract)

2–3 tbsp good-quality apricot jam

75g (3oz) clotted cream

Step one Preheat the oven to 130°C/275°F/gas 1. Put the cream, milk and bay leaves into a saucepan and bring slowly to the boil. Reduce the heat to minimum and leave to infuse, stirring once or twice, for 15 minutes or longer.

Step two Whisk the egg yolks with the sugar until pale and thick. Gradually whisk the hot cream mixture into the egg yolks, then stir in the vanilla extract if you are not using vanilla sugar. Strain into 6 ramekins or small ovenproof bowls, filling them almost, but not quite, to the brim. Stand the dishes in a roasting tin and pour enough hot water around them to come about half way up their sides. Very carefully place in the oven and bake for 45–60 minutes, until just set and slightly crusty. Take out of the roasting tin and leave to cool, then chill for several hours or overnight.

Step three Gently warm the apricot jam, without boiling, until runny. Spread thinly over the surface of each baked custard, then return them to the fridge for 30 minutes. Beat the clotted cream lightly to loosen the consistency, then spoon large dollops on top of the apricot jam and smooth it over even more carefully. Chill again. If you wish, decorate each pot with a bay leaf before serving.

Strawberry and Fresh Angelica Tart

By infusing angelica in the milk for the crème pâtissière, the classic French strawberry tart is elevated into one of the most sublime desserts. You need to make the pâte sablée and crème pâtissière in advance, and try not to hull and halve the strawberries until just before you need them.

Step one For the pastry, sift the flour with the salt and icing sugar. In a food processor, mix together with the butter and egg yolks to form a soft dough. Scrape up into a ball. Knead briefly to smooth out, then wrap in clingfilm and chill for at least 4 hours.

Step two Roll out the pastry and use to line a 25cm (10in) tart tin. If it tears just patch it up with the trimmings. Cover and chill for 1 hour. Preheat the oven to 180°C/350°F/gas 4.

Step three Prick the base of the pastry with a fork. Line with greaseproof paper and weight down with baking beans. Bake blind for 20 minutes, then remove the beans and paper and return the pastry to the oven for a further 15–20 minutes, until lightly browned and crisp. Cool on a rack.

Step four For the crème pâtissière put the milk into a pan with the vanilla, angelica and salt. Bring slowly to the boil, then turn down the heat very low, cover and leave for 30 minutes. (If you can't get a really low flame, take the pan off the heat and set aside.)

Step five Whisk the egg yolks with the sugar until pale. Whisk in the flour. Gradually whisk in the hot milk. Discard the angelica leaves and the vanilla pod. Return the milk mixture to the pan and bring slowly to the boil, whisking to smooth out any lumps. Let it bubble for 1 minute, keeping the heat low and stirring. Draw off the heat and leave until tepid.

Step six As near as possible to serving, spread the crème pâtissière in the pastry case. Arrange the prepared stawberries in concentric circles covering the crème pâtissière. Dust with a little icing sugar and decorate with fresh angelica leaves.

Serves 8

about 1kg (2¼ lb) small strawberries, hulled and halved

icing sugar for dusting

fresh angelica leaves, to garnish

for the pâte sablée

275g (10oz) plain flour

a pinch of salt

110g (4oz) icing sugar

200g (7oz) unsalted butter

2 egg yolks

for the crème pâtissière

350ml (12fl oz) milk

1 vanilla pod

3 or 4 (depending on thickness) 7.5cm (3in) lengths of fresh angelica stems

a pinch of salt

2 egg yolks

50g (2oz) caster sugar

40g (1½ oz) plain flour

Chocolate Meringue Cake with Cherries and Mascarpone

It is a shame that Black Forest gateau has been so bastardized and ruined by commerce, since cherries and chocolate are a natural partnership. Raspberries, too, go blissfully well with chocolate. This chocolate cake, slathered with rich mascarpone and fruit, is even more indulgent than a proper Black Forest gateau. The cake is crisp and meringue-like on the outside and fudgy with chocolate on the inside. All in all, this makes an indecently rich and wicked pudding.

Serves 8

115g (4oz) plain chocolate

115g (4oz) unsalted butter, softened

3 eggs, separated

30g (1oz) plain flour

115g (4oz) caster sugar

to serve

150ml (¼ pint) whipping cream, whipped

225g (8oz) mascarpone

450g (1lb) cherries, stoned, or raspberries

Step one Preheat the oven to 160°C/325°F/gas 3. Line a 19–20cm (7½–8in) cake tin with silver foil, then butter the sides generously and cut a circle of non-stick baking parchment to line the base.

Step two Break the chocolate into squares or chop it in a food processor, place in a bowl above a pan of simmering water and melt it. As soon as it has melted, take the bowl off the heat. Beat in half the butter, a little at a time, and then the egg yolks.

Step three Blend the flour with the remaining butter until soft and evenly mixed and stir into the chocolate mixture until completely amalgamated. Whisk the egg whites until stiff, add half the sugar and whisk again, until shiny and thick. Fold in the remaining sugar. Lightly fold the meringue into the chocolate mixture and pour into the cake tin. Stand the tin in a roasting tin half-filled with hot water and bake for 1½ hours. Remove from the oven and leave to cool. Turn out just before serving.

Step four Fold the whipped cream into the mascarpone. Either pile high on the cake and top with a tumble of cherries or raspberries, or arrange slices of cake on individual plates, with a large dollop of mascarpone cream and a generous mound of fruit scattered over. Devour.

A Summer's Delight

Meringue, cream, strawberries and roses – the very essence of an English summer. Folded together and piled up high, with a deep red coulis of roses drizzled over the sides, this is a show-stopping pudding.

Step one Hull the strawberries and halve, or quarter if large. Put them in a bowl and stir in the sugar and rose water, then cover and leave for at least an hour and up to 4 hours, as long as the room is not too warm. In high summer, leave in the fridge so that they don't start to ferment!

Step two To make the rose coulis, separate the rose petals, removing the white heels if you have the time and inclination, then liquidize with the sugar and orange and lemon juice until smooth.

Step three Just before serving, whip the cream until it just holds its shape, then lightly fold in the strawberry mixture and the pieces of meringue. Pile into individual sundae glasses, drizzle over a little of the rose coulis, then decorate with a sprig of mint and 2 or 3 fresh rose petals. Alternatively, pile into one large crystal bowl, drizzling rose coulis between dollops and letting the last of it trickle down the sides. Scatter with fresh rose petals and serve.

Serves 5–8

500g (1lb 2oz) ripe strawberries

50g (2oz) vanilla sugar

1 tbsp rose water

300ml (½ pint) whipping cream

50g (2oz) meringues, roughly crushed

for the rose coulis

3 fragrant deep pink roses

50g (2oz) caster sugar

2 tbsp orange juice

2 tbsp lemon juice

to decorate

petals of 1 fragrant dark red or deep pink rose

5–6 fresh mint sprigs.

For the ultimate delight, make the meringues yourself. Preheat the oven to 110°C/225°F/gas ¼. Whisk egg whites until they hold their shape, whisk in 25g (1oz) sugar per egg white until glossy, then fold in a further 25g (1oz) sugar per egg white. Dollop onto trays lined with rice paper or non-stick baking parchment and leave in the oven for 1½–1¾ hours, until firm underneath.

Citrus Salad with Warm Lemon Balm Sabayon Sauce

The rich, mousse-like sabayon sauce, scented with lemon balm, turns a rather pure salad of citrus fruit into a luxurious pudding. I like it best when the sabayon is still a little warm, but that means a fair bit of last-minute whisking (an electric whisk is a big help) in the kitchen while your guests wait. If you want to avoid that, it can be made in advance but you'll have to settle for a cold sauce. Either way, serve the salad with crisp shortbread or thin biscuits such as *langues de chat*.

Serves 4

2 oranges

1 pink grapefruit

1 yellow grapefruit

1 lime

6 fresh lemon balm leaves, roughly torn

2 tbsp honey

1 pretty lemon balm sprig, to decorate

for the sabayon sauce

2 egg yolks

25g (1oz) caster sugar

125ml (4fl oz) dry but fragrant white wine

6 fresh lemon balm leaves, chopped

4 tbsp double cream

Step one Using a sharp knife, segment the citrus fruit in the following way: cut off all the peel, slicing just into the flesh, so that none of the white pith remains. Carefully slice down close to the membrane separating each segment on either side, so that the perfectly naked, skinned segments fall out. Place them in a dish with the torn lemon balm leaves, drizzle over the honey and turn carefully. Cover and set aside until needed.

Step two To make the sabayon, put all the ingredients except the cream in a bowl and set it over a pan of simmering water, making sure that the base of the bowl does not touch the water. Whisk continuously using an electric whisk if possible (or a balloon whisk if you have to) until the mixture becomes quite pale and billows up to form a thick, mousse-like cream – this may take up to 10 minutes or even a little longer. Draw off the heat and continue to whisk for a couple more minutes. Add the cream and whisk for a further 20 seconds or so (make that a little longer if you are whisking it by hand). Serve at once with the citrus salad, decorated with the lemon balm sprig.

If you want to avoid last-minute whisking, you can make the sabayon sauce in advance, but when you take it off the heat, and before you add the cream, set the bowl in a bowl full of ice cubes and keep whisking until it is cold. This will prevent it separating. Then add the cream and whisk again briefly. Store, covered, in the fridge, until it is needed.

Moroccan Fig and Pistachio Salad with Rose Water

This has to be one of the prettiest of fruit salads, especially when made with purple-skinned figs, which set off the green pistachios beautifully. To skin pistachios, cover with boiling water, leave for about 30 seconds, then drain and pop them out of their skins.

Step one Arrange the fig quarters on a plate. Warm the honey briefly with the rose water, mixing the two together, then drizzle over the figs.

Step two Scatter with the pistachios, and serve at room temperature, with the cream for those who want it.

Serves 3–4

8 ripe green or purple figs, quartered

1 tbsp honey

2 tsp rose water

15g (½ oz) skinned pistachios, roughly chopped

crème fraîche, double cream or whipped cream, to serve (optional)

Torta di Pesche o Prugne (Peach or Plum Torte)

This big, moist Italian fruit cake is a joy in the summer months when peaches and, later, plums are fragrant and plentiful. Some of the fruit is buried in the pale golden crumb, while the rest, scattered generously over the surface, catches and buckles and caramelizes in the heat of the oven. The torta is relatively thin, in the Italian style, compared to our own cakes, ready to be eaten in large wedges, on its own, or with mascarpone or whipped cream as the fancy takes you. I find that it improves on keeping, so if you can bear to keep it in an airtight container for 24 hours, you will find it worth the wait.

Serves 8–10

400g (14oz) plain flour

1 level tbsp baking powder

310g (11oz) caster sugar

4 eggs

finely grated zest of 1 lemon

150g (5oz) unsalted butter, melted and cooled until tepid

5–6 peaches or nectarines or 8–10 plums, depending on size

cream or mascarpone, to serve (optional)

Step one Preheat the oven to 180°C/350°F/gas 4. Line the base of a 26cm (10½in) cake tin with non-stick baking parchment and butter the sides generously. Sift the flour with the baking powder. Reserve 3 tablespoons of the sugar, then whisk the remainder with the eggs until the mixture is pale and thick. Fold in the flour and the lemon zest, alternating with the melted butter.

Step two Skin the peaches or nectarines, if using, then halve and remove the stones. If using plums, just halve and remove the stones. Cut the fruit into slices about as thick as a £1 coin.

Step three Spoon about half of the cake batter into the prepared tin, and smooth over. Lay about one-third of the fruit higgledy-piggledy over the batter, then dollop on the remaining batter and smooth down lightly. Cover with the rest of the fruit, then sprinkle the reserved sugar over the top. Bake for 55–60 minutes or until a skewer inserted into the centre comes out clean (except maybe for a smear of molten fruit).

Step four Turn out onto a wire rack, and leave to cool. Serve in big wedges; it's lovely on its own and devilishly good as a pudding, with cream or mascarpone.

The Ultimate Pumpkin Pie

This recipe for pumpkin pie was given to me many years ago by Frances Bendixon, and it's still the one I use every autumn.

Step one Preheat the oven to 190°C/375°F/gas 5. Place the pumpkin on an oiled baking sheet, cut-sides down, cover with foil and bake in the oven until soft (this could take up to 2½ hours).

Step two Leave the cooked pumpkin to cool, then scoop out the pulp and whizz in a food processor until smooth. Tip into a colander lined with a double layer of muslin and leave to drain overnight to eliminate any wateriness.

Step three Next day, sift the flour with the salt. Rub the butter into the flour until it resembles fine breadcrumbs. Make a well in the centre and add the egg yolk and enough iced water to form a soft dough. Mix quickly and lightly, and knead very briefly until smooth. Wrap and chill for at least 30 minutes. Bring it back to room temperature before using.

Step four Place a baking sheet in the oven and preheat to 220°C/425°F/gas 7. Line a deep 23cm (9in) pie plate or tart tin with the pastry. Use a fork to decorate the rim. Prick the base with a fork and chill until needed.

Step five Beat the eggs, then beat in the pumpkin purée, followed by the spices, salt and cream. Add the maple syrup gradually, tasting as you do so (if you use a sweet squash, you may not need all of it). Add extra spices to taste then pour the mixture into the pastry case.

Step six Place the filled case on the hot baking sheet in the oven. Bake for 10 minutes to start the crust browning, then reduce the heat to 190°C/375°F/gas 5. Cook for about 30 minutes or until the filling looks set around the edges and about halfway to the middle of the pie, but the centre is still a bit wobbly. Serve warm or cold.

Serves 6–8

1.25kg (2lb 12oz) wedge of pumpkin (or other winter squash, or 3 large butternut squashes), cut in half, seeds and fibres removed

oil, for greasing

2 large eggs

1½ tsp ground cinnamon

½ tsp ground ginger

½ tsp ground allspice

½ tsp salt

250ml (9fl oz) double cream

125ml (4fl oz) maple syrup, or to taste

for the pastry

225g (8oz) plain flour

pinch of salt

115g (4oz) chilled butter, diced

1 beaten yolk

iced water

Margaret Pover's Moist Lemon Cake

Mrs Pover, who runs an immaculate bed and breakfast between her bouts of cake-making, reckons that a brace of these lovely, syrupy, sharp lemon cakes will set her back little more than £4. She has been making them all summer long, so she can recite the recipe from memory and no longer needs to look up quantities. In a matter of minutes she whizzes up a new batch of batter and it's straight into the oven. Her cakes usually get eaten up pretty swiftly, but if needs be they will keep particularly well in an airtight container in a cool place.

Serves 8

175g (6oz) caster sugar

175g (6oz) self-raising flour

175g (6oz) softened butter

1 level tsp baking powder

3 medium eggs

finely grated zest of 1 large lemon

75ml (3fl oz) milk

To finish

3 tbsp granulated sugar, plus a little extra

juice of 1 large lemon

a few curls of lemon zest

Step one Preheat the oven to 180°C/350°F/gas 4. Line the base of a 18–20cm (7–8in) cake tin with non-stick baking parchment and grease the sides. Put all the ingredients for the cake into a food processor and process until smooth and evenly mixed, to produce a fairly runny cake batter. Pour into the prepared tin and bake for 40–50 minutes, until a skewer inserted in the centre comes out clean.

Step two While the cake is in the oven, make the lemon syrup by stirring the 3 tablespoons of sugar into the lemon juice until dissolved. Once the cake is cooked, let it stand in the tin for 5 minutes, then turn out on to a plate. With a fine skewer, pierce a dozen or so holes in the cake. Pour this syrup over the cake once it has been turned out and pierced. Sprinkle the top with a thin, even layer of granulated sugar and then finish with a few extra curls of lemon zest scattered prettily over the top.

Blackberry and Apple Compote with Star Anise

Gather blackberries while the going is good in late summer and early autumn before the frosts perish them. To stretch them out a little, partner with new season's apples (eaters, not cookers, please) to make a wonderful old-fashioned blackberry and apple compote. I love the hint of aniseed imparted by the star anise, but they are entirely optional. Any leftover compote is lovely for breakfast, eaten with large dollops of Greek-style yoghurt.

Step one Put all the ingredients in a non-reactive saucepan and add about 50ml (2fl oz) water. Cover and cook over a low heat for 5 minutes, until the dark blackberry juice begins to ooze out, stirring once or twice to dissolve the sugar.

Step two Simmer until the slices of apple are very tender. Serve hot, warm or cold.

Serves 8–10

900g (2 lb) blackberries

10 good eating apples, peeled, cored and sliced

500g (1lb 2oz) caster sugar

2 cinnamon sticks

2 star anise
(or 4 cloves)

Le Progrès au Chocolat

Make the hazelnut meringue the evening before serving the Progrès au Chocolat, or first thing in the morning, to give the discs time to cool.

Serves 8

225g (8oz) hazelnuts, toasted and skinned

350g (12oz) caster sugar

25g (1oz) cornflour

6 large egg whites

a pinch of salt

¼ tsp cream of tartar

1 tsp vanilla essence

a little cocoa powder, for dusting

for the chocolate cream

200g (7oz) good-quality plain chocolate, broken into squares

a small knob of butter

300ml (½ pint) double cream, whipped

Step one Preheat the oven to 110°C/225°F/gas ¼. Cut out 3 sheets of non-stick baking parchment to line 3 baking sheets. Draw a 20cm (8in) circle on each one, using a plate as a template. Lay the paper, pencil marks downwards, on the baking sheets.

Step two Grind the toasted hazelnuts to a fine powder in a food processor. Mix with 225g (8oz) of the sugar and all the cornflour.

Step three Whisk the egg whites until foamy. Add the salt and cream of tartar and continue whisking until the whites form soft peaks. A spoonful at a time, beat in the remaining sugar until you have stiff, glossy peaks. Whisk in the vanilla essence. Gradually fold in the nut mixture working fast to retain as much air as possible.

Step four Spread one-third of the mixture over each circle, forming a disc 1cm (½in) thick. Bake for 1–1½ hours, until firm and dry to the touch. Lift each meringue to check if the underneath is firm and dry. If not, cook for a further 20 minutes or so until done. Leaving the meringues in the oven, turn off the heat and close the door. Leave to cool completely before taking them out. (If time is short you can cool them more quickly on racks but they are far more likely to crack.)

Step five Place the chocolate in a bowl set over a pan of gently simmering water (or cover the bowl tightly and microwave at half power in 1-minute bursts). As soon as it has melted, draw off the heat and beat in the knob of butter. Cool until tepid, then fold in the whipped cream.

Step six Carefully sandwich the 3 hazelnut meringue discs together with the chocolate cream and keep cool. Dust lightly with cocoa just before serving.

Pear and Cranberry Oat Crisp

A crisp, in this particular sweet-toothed sense of the word, is an American version of crumble. This one combines pears and all-American cranberries. Out of cranberry season, add another pear and reduce the sugar a little.

Step one Preheat the oven to 190°C/375°F/gas 5.

Step two Mix the pears, cranberries, cinnamon, cloves and caster sugar together and tip into a shallow ovenproof dish – I use a round dish 23cm (9in) in diameter.

Step three For the topping, mix the flour with the oats and salt. Rub in the butter until the mixture resembles coarse breadcrumbs, then stir in the sugar. Scatter the crisp crumbs over the fruit in a thick, even blanket. Bake for 30–40 minutes, until browned and bubbling. Serve hot or warm.

Serves 4

3 pears, peeled, cored and thickly sliced

110g (4oz) cranberries

1 tsp ground cinnamon

3 cloves

75g (3oz) caster sugar

for the topping

175g (6oz) plain flour

50g (2oz) rolled oats

a pinch of salt

75g (3oz) butter, diced

150g (5oz) caster sugar

Have you made this recipe? Tell us what you think at
www.mykitchentable.co.uk/blog

Thyme Sorbet

A white wine sorbet scented with thyme is amazingly good. Serve it as part of a selection of sorbets and ice creams, or scooped into small melon halves to refresh on a hot summer's day. The recipe comes from the very best guide to ice-cream making, *Ices* by Caroline Liddell and Robin Weir.

Serves 6–8

500g (1lb 2oz) sugar

7g (¼ oz) or 4 x 5cm (2in) thyme sprigs

225ml (8fl oz) dry white wine

2 tbsp lemon juice

Step one First make the sugar syrup. Put the sugar into a saucepan over a medium heat and add 450ml (16fl oz) water. Stir until the sugar has dissolved to make clear syrup. Draw off the heat and leave to cool. Then measure 450ml (16fl oz) into another pan and add the thyme.

Step two Pour in 225ml (8fl oz) water and bring slowly to the boil. Draw off the heat and add the wine. Cover and leave to cool. Chill overnight.

Step three Add the lemon juice and strain. If you have an ice-cream machine, freeze the sorbet in that.

Step three (alternative) If not, pour the mixture into a shallow freezer container and pop into the freezer, turned to its coldest setting. Leave until the edges are solid but the centre still liquid. Break up the edges and push them into the centre. Return to the freezer and repeat once. Now leave until the sorbet is set right through but not yet rock hard, then scrape the contents of the container into a food processor and quickly process to smooth out jagged ice crystals. Scrape the mush back into the container and return post-haste to the freezer. If you don't have a food processor you'll have to beat the sorbet with all your might to break down the crystals. Now leave until fully set.

Step four Transfer from the freezer to the fridge to 'ripen' – or, in other words, soften – about 20–25 minutes before serving.

Any leftover syrup can be stored, almost indefinitely, in a sealed jar in the fridge.

10 9 8 7 6 5 4 3 2 1

Published in 2012 by BBC Books, an imprint of Ebury Publishing. A Random House Group company.

Recipes © Sophie Grigson 2012
Book design © Woodlands Books Ltd 2012

All recipes contained in this book first appeared in *Eat Your Greens* (1993), *Herbs* (1999), *Feasts for a Fiver* (1999), *Sunshine Food* (2000) and *My Favourite Family Recipes* (2003).

Sophie Grigson has asserted her right to be identified as the author of this Work in accordance with the Copyright, Designs and Patents Act 1988

The Random House Group Limited
Reg. No. 954009

A CIP catalogue record for this book is available from the British Library

The Random House Group Limited supports The Forest Stewardship Council (FSC®), the leading international forest certification organisation. Our books carrying the FSC label are printed on FSC® certified paper. FSC is the only forest certification scheme endorsed by the leading environmental organisations, including Greenpeace. Our paper procurement policy can be found at www.randomhouse.co.uk/environment

Addresses for companies within the Random House Group can be found at www.randomhouse.co.uk

To buy books by your favourite authors and register for offers visit www.randomhouse.co.uk

Printed and bound in the UK by Butler, Tanner and Dennis Ltd
Colour origination by AltaImage

Commissioning Editor: Muna Reyal
Project Editor: Joe Cottington
Designer: Lucy Stephens
Photographer: William Reavell © Woodlands Books Ltd 2012 (see also credits below)
Food Stylists:: Lyn Rutherford, Maxine Clark, Annie Nichols, Denise Smart, Laura Fyfe, Mari Williams and Katie Giovanni
Prop Stylists: Roisin Nield and Wei Tang
Front cover location: jj Locations
Copy Editor: Anne McDowall
Production: Rebecca Jones

Photography on p4 Noel Murphy © Woodlands Books Ltd 2012; pages 9, 18, 22, 37, 38, 74, 77, 78, 81, 86, 89, 90, 93, 114, 117, 118, 121, 149, 158, 178, 181, 182, 185, 186, 189 and 194 © Jean Koppel; pages 41, 42, 45, 82, 85, 113, 122, 125, 126, 150, 153, 154, 157, 190 and 193 © Georgia Glynn-Smith.

ISBN: 9781849903998

MIX
Paper from
responsible sources
FSC® C023561